National Congress on Languages in Education

THE MOTHER TONGUE AND OTHER LANGUAGES IN EDUCATION

NCLE Papers and Reports 2

The second of two volumes of papers from Working Parties
for the First Assembly, Durham, 1978

Edited by G.E. Perren

Centre for Information on Language Teaching and Research

First published 1979
© 1979 Centre for Information on Language Teaching and Research
ISBN 0 903466 23 6
Printed in Great Britain by Staples Printing Group
Published by the Centre for Information on Language Teaching and Research,
20 Carlton House Terrace, London SW1Y 5AP

Contents

Introduction

The National Congress on Languages in Education originated from an agreement in 1974, between representatives of a number of professional associations and organisations concerned with the teaching and study of languages at all levels of education in Britain, to establish a national forum for discussion with machinery for studying and reporting on matters of common interest. It was envisaged that the work of the Congress should be continuous and would be carried on by means of working parties of experts which would be asked to study and report on particular problems. Reports by the working parties would be presented at biennial Assemblies to representatives from all the associations and organisations supporting the Congress. Each Assembly would, in its turn, then identify and recommend subjects for new working parties leading up to the next Assembly.

In 1976 two working parties were set up to report to the first Assembly to be held in 1978. As over 30 associations and organisations had by then declared their general support for the Congress, these working parties consisted not only of a nucleus of experts, invited to serve as individuals, but also included a number of consultants who might be nominated by any of the constituent organisations wishing to be associated with their work. Administrative and secretarial services for the working parties — and indeed for the whole Congress organisation — was provided by the Centre for Information on Language Teaching and Research.

It was desirable that, initially at any rate, subjects to be studied by working parties should be of interest to as many of the constituent associations as possible, as well as being issues on which they would be able to make genuine and valuable contributions to current educational policy and practice.

Thus working party 1 (chairman: Professor E.W. Hawkins) was asked to study *The priorities to be accorded to non-native languages at all levels of education in Britain* — a subject which clearly affected all teachers of foreign languages as well as having important administrative implications. Working party 2 (chairman: Professor A. Spicer) was asked to study *The relationship between the acquisition/teaching of the mother-tongue and the learning/teaching of other languages* — a subject with significant but often neglected psychological and pedagogical implications for teachers of English as well as of foreign languages. Both the subjects chosen concerned the curriculum as a whole as well as language teaching in particular; both seemed appropriate at a time when the general content and organisation of secondary education was under intensive review. Neither was to be concerned merely with techniques of teaching and both were attempting tasks hitherto not tackled on a broad scale.

Inevitably and desirably perhaps there were areas of possible overlap between the two fields of work, and it was necessary to ensure that each group should be continuously aware of the activities of the other. This, however, presented little difficulty since interim reports and papers were circulated to both and there was good liaison. While some differences of emphasis arose from their different approaches to some common problems, any general educational principles which emerged from the deliberations of both working parties seemed remarkably congruent.

1

In the event neither working party felt that it was able to produce a collective report on its chosen subject, but for the first Assembly in July 1978 each therefore provided a number of papers, written by individuals but approved by the group, dealing with various aspects of their subject. These papers, edited and revised, now provide the content of two volumes published by CILT as *Foreign languages in education* and *The mother tongue and other languages in education*.

The present volume thus consists of papers prepared by members of working party 2 and its consultants. Some have been extensively revised since they were first presented. Three of the original papers are not included because they have been published elsewhere: J. and S. McDonough, *Teaching English as a foreign language and mother tongue teaching* in the *Educational Review*, November 1978, and two papers on Welsh and Gaelic in *The older mother tongues of the United Kingdom*, CILT, 1978.

Working party 2 had very wide general terms of reference. Its subject moreover was one which had seldom been discussed as a central educational issue, while specialist debates on points of detail had more often than not led to disagreement between teachers of English as a mother tongue and teachers of foreign languages. Often the two groups had shown little concern about each other's work, aims and results. Some decades ago, when the teaching of grammar was regarded as an acceptable aim in English and an essential objective in foreign language teaching, there had been disputes about which side should introduce grammatical concepts, nomenclature, etc, which both needed. Agreement in principle (in 1910) dissolved into divergence in practice. When, later, teachers of English abjured grammar, teachers of foreign languages were left with an awkward child of dubious parentage. More recently, of course there has been a revival of interest on the part of English teachers in basic linguistic concepts, some of which are highly relevant to foreign language teaching. In any case the more linguistically sophisticated the *learner* is made by his teachers, the more he himself will seek to coordinate and correlate whatever he has learned about the underlying structure of his mother tongue and any other languages he is taught.

However, there had been two comparatively recent meetings on the relationship between teaching the mother tongue and a foreign language. In 1973 CILT had convened a conference whose papers and findings were published under the rather ominous title *The space between* (CILT, 1974), and a seminar had been sponsored by the British Association for Applied Linguistics in 1976, whose papers had been circulated with the aid of a grant from the Nuffield Foundation (BAAL, 1977). The working party was indebted to these previous discussions, on which it sought to build. Since several of its members had been party to them, it did not start completely cold.

It was at once recognised that the example of Wales was of outstanding interest to the working party. There English and Welsh were both being taught as mother tongues and as foreign languages; to a smaller degree a similar case existed in the west of Scotland in respect of Gaelic and English. Since authoritative information about both areas was provided by consultants, which deserved extensive treatment — not least because so many teachers in England appeared remarkably uninformed about them — it was decided to publish this in a separate volume, *The older mother tongues of the United Kingdom* (James, 1978). This forms an essential complement to the present collection, dealing as it does with the only areas in Britain where administrative and political necessity now *requires* the teaching of the mother tongue and of a foreign language to be coordinated.

Early in its discussions the working party was made aware of dangers in assuming any community of interest between teachers of English and teachers of other languages where demonstrably none was felt. It was warned that bridges could not be built if suitable foundations for them did not exist and that among school teachers good fences might make good neighbours; that while both English and modern languages claimed to have inherited some of the educational values once attributed to the classics, they had since pursued very different social and curricular aims. English, for example, had not only undertaken its original Arnoldian task of transmitting traditional cultural values to those in school, but by its nature had felt the duty and necessity of creating new ones, consonant with the changes in the school population, the spirit of the age and the mundane task of speading literacy itself. Thus English had a vastly more responsible task educationally than that ascribed to foreign languages — that is of merely implanting the mechanics of communication to a degree which would not permit cultural participation and at best could only provide complementary or contrastive literary values at second hand. To some it may seem a long journey from Arnold's 'preachers of culture' (at the philistine middle classes of his day) to contemporary teachers of English who, while overtly rejecting such 'élitism', still stoutly maintain the moral purpose of their subject. Nevertheless, the essential evangelism of English teaching has persisted. Differences in 'subject philosophy' of this kind sometimes made it difficult to express aims and objectives in a similar or comparable way. English teachers, it appeared, could not subscribe to any single statement about their classroom objectives: their subject was too wide and too pervasive. While 'modern languages' could to some extent express their unity of purpose through a common methodology, any such cohesive factor was unlikely to be found among teachers of English as a mother tongue — or if one was deduced, it would be spurious. Teachers of foreign languages, it seemed, were much more concerned to develop a common party line than teachers of English, possibly because they were far less sure of their place in the curriculum. On the one hand there was certainly no fear that English might disappear from the curriculum, although it might perhaps become so widely dispersed and diluted *across* the curriculum as to become less a subject and more a way of life. On the other, foreign languages might conceivably disappear from the school timetable altogether, or at best become confined to such selective strong points which might yet withstand the onslaught of the neo-philistines in comprehensive education.

Despite such differences at the doctrinal level, pragmatically much of common interest emerged. As educationists all were deeply concerned about current short-comings in the training and education of teachers: as language specialists all were aware of a central need for a sound foundation of psycho- and socio-linguistic theory equally applicable to all language learning and teaching. In matters of methodology it was accepted that teachers of the mother tongue and of foreign languages had

3

much they could learn from one another — without prejudice to their agreed differences in aims.

The working party was, of course not only concerned with relationships between English and the orthodox foreign languages commonly taught in school. The relationship between *any* mother tongue and *any* foreign language were equally its business. Welsh and Gaelic could be dealt with primarily as regional special cases, but the newer mother tongues of Britain — the languages of many widely located minority groups — and their relationship to education and the teaching of English (as a foreign language) had to be considered as part of the total pattern of British education. Not only was this an aspect of a comparatively new educational phenomenon on which no clear previous views existed, but it was one which conveniently reversed the role of English in making it the principal *foreign* language to be considered rather than the archetypal mother tongue.

The following papers fairly represent both the points of contact and the divergencies which were resolved. Collectively they may well provide good bases for a continuing dialectic which will become more and more necessary in a society where social cohesion must transcend linguistic diversity or educational separatism.

Chapter 1 begins by examining a number of propositions, primarily at the level of psycholinguistics, relating the learning of both mother tongue and foreign language. It has, however, important implications for classroom methodology. It notes the complexity of the language teaching problems in Britain today, and points out that with more research this 'should lead to a coherent theory of second language learning, rather than the heterogeneous assortment of ideas which we have today.'

Chapter 2 consists of two parts. In the first, Rosen provides an historical review which goes far to explain how the present extreme variety of attitudes to teaching English as a mother tongue in Britain had descended from many different interpretations of the traditions, responsibilities and social purpose of the subject. In the second part, Stratta examines some of these attitudes in detail relating them to the content and methodology of teaching. In passing, it might be observed that some of these 'approaches' are not of course confined to specialist teachers of English. A 'radical/political' approach (see page 35) can be, and often is, seen in such subjects as science and more particularly history.

Chapter 3 is concerned with the place of mother tongues other than English, Welsh or Gaelic in the educational development of Britain. It contrasts the protective and indulgent attitude of the English towards their own mother tongue — based on the best educational principles — with the rather less sympathetic view taken towards the newer mother tongues of Britain, probably because of historical and social factors.

In Chapter 4 Hawkins argues the case for a new curriculum subject — 'language' — which would be not merely another name for another approach to English, but which could become the basis for the appreciation of all languages as characteristic forms of human behaviour. His criticism of the Bullock Report's proposals — that if language is spread across the curriculum it might then become no-one's specific responsibility — would be supported by many teachers of English. Unlike them however, he would involve the teachers of foreign languages as well as teachers of English in the development and presentation of the new subject.

Chapters 5 and 6 provide two contrastive studies of practices in other countries which may be found instructive. Dawson analyses official directives and classroom practice in France, where, of course, conscience about the role of language in education has always been highly valued. Burstall describes current aims and procedures in assessing language performance in North America. At a time when there is much talk of re-establishing 'standards' in Britain by periodic tests and assessments of performance, she rightly draws attention to some of the dangers attendant on the notion of public 'accountability' by teachers or schools.

The final chapter is a composite review of the state of teacher education and training related to both teachers of English and teachers of foreign languages. Mittins analyses closely the claims to professional status of teachers of English — but much of what he says applies equally to teachers of other languages. (His view should be compared with those of Rosen and Stratta in chapter 2.) Spicer and Dawson describe in detail the shortcoming of the present preparation of foreign language teachers — and much of this could also apply to teachers of English. The proposals for amelioration by better in-service training are precise and practical. The longer-term suggestions for the linguistic education of all language teachers emphasise the importance of adequate studies in the teacher's and pupil's mother tongue as a basis for teaching and learning a foreign language.

The reader of these papers will observe that they collectively further the belief that teachers of the mother tongue and teachers of foreign languages should not only be fully aware of each others' aims and work, but should share aspects of their training to such an extent that some, at any rate, would become fully qualified to teach both. It is at the level of classroom teaching that such coordination would be most valuable and at present is most difficult to ensure.

References

BAAL: British Association for Applied Linguistics. *Languages for life*. Papers from the BAAL seminar held at La Sainte Union College of Higher Education, Southampton, 13–15 December 1976. BAAL, 1977.

Centre for Information on Language Teaching and Research. CILT Reports and Papers 10: *The space between: English and foreign languages at school*. CILT, 1974.

James, C.V., ed. *The older mother tongues of the United Kingdom*. CILT, 1978. The two long papers *Welsh*, by Eric Evans and *Scottish Gaelic* by Murdo MacLeod provide not only useful historical surveys but detailed information about the teaching of the languages in schools today. There is also a short section by H.G. McRory on *Irish Gaelige* in Northern Ireland. Together they provide full case studies of the only examples of a bilingual education policy within Britain in maintained schools.

1. First and second language learning

V.J. Cook,
J. Long and
S. McDonough

Discussions of languages in education usually concern themselves with why we should teach languages, what we should teach, and how we should teach them, but are rarely concerned with how people *learn* languages. Yet, if these discussions are to have any effect on education, they must at some stage be related to language learning. The purpose of this paper is to draw attention to some of the issues about language learning that need to be remembered when considering the other contributions to this volume.

Thus we are concerned here with language learning in an educational context. The basis is the research evidence about language learning that has been built up during the last two decades. The argument is put in terms of the comparison of the child learning a first language and the foreigner learning a second, henceforth abbreviated to L1 and L2 learning. For many years the question has been debated whether L2 learning is the same as L1 learning. Phrased in this way the question is impossible to answer since it reduces a complex issue to a matter of 'Yes' or 'No'; language learning has many aspects, each of which may be similar or different in L1 and L2. The overall position taken here is that there is indeed a fundamental similarity between L1 and L2 learning but, that as soon as we look at language learning in a classroom, there are important differences that have to be taken into account, some of them inescapable, some of them avoidable. Although much of the evidence supports this position (Macnamara, 1976; McLaughlin, 1977), the limitations of the evidence mean that it cannot yet be considered to be proved. So the bulk of this paper provides on the one hand an overview of L1 learning, and on the other hand some ways in which this relates to L2 learning in a classroom; it does not, however, consider the implications of L1 learning for the teaching of the mother tongue. Nevertheless the broad trend of its arguments provides interesting support for some of the main ideas in the paper by Rosen and Stratta (see chapter 2).

First of all it is necessary to draw attention to some general factors involved in the comparison of L1 and L2 learning. One factor is that the settings of L1 learning may be rather different from those of L2 learning. An aspect of this is the number of people the learner meets; while the native child is limited to parents, family, and friends, the L2 learner may encounter one native speaker or teacher at a time, or several. Consequently the kinds of relationship the L2 learner has with the people he meets may be wider than those of the L1 learner. Also the type of exposure to the language will vary; in L2 learning it may range from accidental or even random to highly structured, while in L1 learning it is limited by the ways in which children are brought up in a particular culture and by the adult's beliefs about how they should talk to children. This exposure may vary also in density; in the first language exposure is fairly constant, in the second language it can vary from occasional to regular (but widely spaced) to 'immersion'. In short then, the settings in which L2 learning takes place are more varied than for L1 learning.

7

As well as settings, another important factor is the learner. Second languages are learnt later than first languages and so L2 learners are usually older than L1 learners. Though this may seem an obvious point, nevertheless it needs stating that charac- teristics associated with growing older, such as more mature cognitive and emotional development, must inevitably be expected to affect L2 learning. It has often been suggested, for instance, that teenagers and adults can use more conscious mental processing than the intuitive processing of the child (Krashen, 1977) and in the emotional sphere it is sometimes felt that the differences between what a learner wants to say in an L2 and what he can say in his L1 is frustrating in a way similar to the pressure on the native child to communicate. In addition L2 learners have rather different motivations and attitudes from L1 learners, even if it is hard to say exactly what motivates a child to learn his first language. Finally, L2 learners have often learnt to read and write in their first language and this causes them to approach language learning in a different way.

Having made these general points, we can look at some actual points of comparison between L1 and L2 learning. The structure of the remainder of this paper consists of eight statements about L1 learning. These eight all reflect a reasonable consensus of opinion among those carrying out research into language development within more or less the psycholinguistic tradition. Naturally there are other statements that could be made that are also supported by the evidence. The reason for choosing these eight is that they seem to have potential implications for languages in education. So, after each statement has been elaborated, it is compared with L2 learning and some implications for L2 teaching are drawn. While the argument is based on research findings wherever possible, the general caveat must be made that often the research that bears upon particular points of interest to the language teacher is limited or non- existent; for the purposes of this paper we have sometimes felt it necessary to make certain intuitive leaps beyond our actual state of knowledge.

The child's language is a system in its own right rather than being a small fragment of the adult system

It is a common assumption in work on L1 learning that the child's language system is a system in its own right rather than an incomplete version of the adult system. The child does not as it were, choose bits out of the adult system and add the bits together till he has the complete system; rather he has a system of his own whose bits do not necessarily correspond to the bits of the adult system, even though the system as a whole evolves into it. L1 learning is not so much a matter of adding parts of the adult system one at a time as of developing more and more complex systems that gradually grow to resemble the adult's. So the child seems to have his own grammatical rules (Braine, 1976; Brown, 1973), his own set of language functions (Halliday, 1975) and his own semantic meanings (Clark, 1973), all of which change ultimately into the adult system; it has, however, been questioned whether this is true of phonology (Smith, 1973).

Almost the same assumption has been held by many people studying L2 learning (Selinker, 1972; Nemser, 1971; Corder, 1967). The learner speaks an 'interlanguage'

8

which has a system of its own, different from either the first or second language. This interlanguage, like the child's system, is constantly changing and developing towards the target language; however, unlike the child, a second language learner more often than not fails to develop his system completely into the target and it becomes 'fossilised' at some intermediate point. But, while this 'interlanguage' assumption applies to second language learning in a natural setting, most language teaching has implicitly assumed exactly the opposite; an L2 learner is expected to have a system that is some fragment of the native system, not a system in its own right, and he is required to learn the language bit by bit. For instance in learning English as a foreign language the learner may be first taught the present tense, then the present-continuous, then the past tense, and so on; each of these tenses corresponds to part of the target language and after he has covered them all the learner will have pieced together the tense system of English; he is not, however, allowed to develop a progressively more complicated system of tenses of his own as the native child does. This reliance in the classroom on teaching bits of the target language in an incremental fashion is as true of other aspects of language such as functions as it is of grammar. There may well be factors in the classroom setting that necessitate this approach of 'rule isolation' (Krashen, 1976) but we should be aware that it is very different from either L1 or L2 learning in natural settings.

The learning of a first language has many sides and is not simply a matter of learning syntax and vocabulary

A child learning his first language is evidently learning a number of things besides language forms, some of which are acquired through the medium of the newly learnt language, and some of which lead to further acquisition of the language code. His language is involved in his developing cognitive structure, emotional states, relationships, and play.

A child begins by having a limited set of functions (Halliday, 1975) or things he can do in his language, which are associated with certain classes of expressions, and these are isolated from each other by features such as words or intonation contours. For Halliday, the process of language development consists, besides the elaboration of syntax, in the gradual integration of these language functions, and their replacement by the flexibility of the adult language. In particular this highlights the social role of language. Even very young children use a kind of language in their relationships and play with peers. Work on conversational competence (Keenan, 1974) showed that a young child uses language to get attention from, to play with, and direct other children. This work showed that interaction between children even at the earliest stages is genuine social interplay through language, and not simultaneous or uncoordinated monologues.

In a second language context, the applicability of the statements depends on the characteristics of the learners and the situation. It seems unlikely that the second language will be involved in the pupil's emotional life (except in situations created by its presence, or the need to learn it), nor in his relationships, unless engineered (e.g. pen-friends and foreign visits). Where there is a genuine purpose behind the foreign

9

language in the curriculum, the L2 learner is not simply learning a new syntax and vocabulary, but also how to function in the new language. On the other hand, he is not learning a totally new conceptual system, nor a new set of language functions. Of course, new concepts will arise both from the language and the culture associated with it. But usually depending on the educational purpose, the learner will be acquiring a set of skills to do a job with, and/or a new way of looking at the world derived from the new culture. How much of either he gains will depend on his needs and interests.

If the new language material is perceived by the learner to be relevant to his goal, and if the types of social interaction conducted in the new language are varied, then L2 learning may share some of the rich and multi-faceted nature of L1. A move toward language courses that capitalise both on the range of communicative functions an L2 learner can use his first language for, and on the L2 learner's expectation of the range of functions he may need his second language for, is represented by the Council of Europe's project for a unit credit scheme (Trim, 1974) and by the work on English for specific purposes. These are based on the hypothesis that motivation will depend on the learner's perception of the function of the new language in his foreseeable future. In general language courses in schools, the lack of a specific focus could, for example, be offset by increasing the relevance of the foreign language work to the mother tongue teaching and the language problems throughout the curriculum.

The use of the first language goes hand in hand with the child's needs and interests

Though perhaps a truism, it needs restating that the child's use of his first language reflects his own world—what he wants to do through language, what he wants to say through language, how he perceives the world, and how he is discovering his social roles. So his first attempts to use language reflect his need to interact with the people around him (Bruner, 1975), his language functions reflect his social relationships. In terms of subject matter, from his first word to his teens he, hardly surprisingly, talks about what interests him (Nelson 1973; Rutherford, Freeth and Mercer, 1970). This is not of course to deny that these needs and interests may be themselves the products of how other children and adults see the child, or of socialisation.

The same statement will of necessity be true of much second language learning in a 'natural' setting; the learner's language reflects his own needs and interests, though these may be different from those of the child. The statement will also be true of classroom L2 learning when it occurs in a situation where the learners have to make immediate use of the language outside the classroom; immigrants for instance obviously need to be taught the ways in which they can put language to practical use. However, the statement has much less application to teaching situations where the language does not have an immediate practical value — the typical situation say of a foreign language classroom in England. For instance, if we teach students how to buy aspirins in France, this may be extremely useful on some future occasion when they are in France, but it is hardly relevant to the headache they have today. Thus, the functional approach commended in the last section is valuable when we can predict what needs the student will have for the foreign language at some future date but is less applicable to classroom situations where we have little idea what use the students will have for the language, if any. In a sense this functional approach shifts the student's needs to the future rather than the immediate present; it is not what the student wants to do today that counts but what he can do tomorrow. This is markedly different not only from L1 learning which starts from today's needs, but also from the progress in 'natural' second language learning which starts from the learner's actual need to function in a conversation *now* (Hatch).

Language teachers might at least consider the alternative of starting from the student's social and psychological needs in the classroom rather than from the student's needs in the future, particularly as it has been shown that in school learners the 'integrative' motivation in which the learner wants to form part of a group through the new language is more powerful than the 'instrumental' motivation in which the learner wants to do things through the language (Gardner, Smythe and Gliksman, 1976).

Whenever there is a relationship between cognition and language development, language depends on cognition

It has always been a matter of controversy how language development is connected with cognitive development. The position adopted here is based on that taken in Cromer's review of the issues involved (1976), namely that, while some aspects of language are independent of cognitive development, other aspects depend on the prior acquisition of certain cognitive abilities. In other words language development does not always depend on thought, but, when the two *are* related, thought usually comes first. So work within Piagetian framework has shown how it is possible to relate language to the child's stage of cognitive development: the two-word stage at one end of development may depend on cognitive schema the child acquires during the earlier 'sensori-motor' stage (Sinclair, 1971); the use of certain syntactic structures by children at about the age of seven may depend upon the acquisition of ideas about 'conservation' (Sinclair 1969).

With the transition to Piaget's stage of 'formal operations' in the teens it becomes a more open question whether language development is the cause rather than the effect of some aspects of cognitive development (Bruner, 1975). But it should not be forgotten that other aspects of language development are independent of cognition. The stages of syntactic development for instance do not correspond particularly well with cognitive stages. Also the kinds of organisation in language may be so different from those in other areas of cognition that it is hard to find points of contact. In case of misapprehension it should be pointed out that 'cognition' is used here in the sense of underlying mental system rather than particular 'concepts'; the statement does not deny that particular concepts are acquired through language but claims rather that, at least until the teens, the underlying cognitive system has an effect on language development rather than vice versa.

The relationship of this statement to L2 learning depends upon the earlier point

11

that the L2 learner is usually at a later stage of cognitive development than the L1 learner. Indeed the differences between older and younger L2 learners have sometimes been explained in terms of increased cognitive maturity (Rosansky, 1976; Tremaine, 1975).

Wherever language depends on cognition we would therefore expect to find difference between L1 and L2 learning regardless of whether the learners are in 'natural' settings. Take the effects of cognition on the order of language acquisition. Statement 6 below considers the order of acquisition in more detail but here it can be pointed out that wherever a point of language depends on cognition we can expect it to be learnt earlier by L2 learners than by L1 learners because the L2 learner already possesses the necessary cognitive structures. Padilla for instance has shown that child L2 learners go through the same order of acquisition of some grammatical morphemes when they are close to the age of the L1 learners, but go through a different order when they are older; in other words, the older children's order of acquisition in the second language is affected by their cognitive and social development.

The application of this statement to language teaching suggests that the grading and sequencing of language in the classroom needs to reflect the cognitive stage of the learner. For instance, there may be some grammatical structures that are learnt late by native children for cognitive reasons. On the one hand, if the L2 learner is still below the appropriate stage there is not much point in teaching these because he won't be able to learn them. On the other hand, if he is past that cognitive stage, they can be introduced much sooner than in L1 learning. The L2 teacher can take for granted the possession of certain concepts. While the teacher of the mother tongue is faced with the tricky problem of deciding whether to teach language as a way to acquiring concepts or to teach concepts as a way to acquiring language, the foreign language teacher can assume to some extent that his students have the underlying conceptual structures.

The child's use and learning of language is partly determined by mental capacity

Mental capacity is used to refer to all internal psychological processes, including those of attention, organisation and memory. Capacity is obviously limited both for the child and the adult but the limitations for the child are more severe. The child, for example, may be less able to direct and sustain its attention (Kagan and Lewis, 1965). Research also suggests that the child's spontaneous attempts to remember verbal materials are less likely to involve typical adult strategies of organisation, such as labelling, clustering, and using covert speech for rehearsal (Hagen, 1971; Bousfield, Esterson and Whitmarsh, 1958; Flavell, Beach and Chinsky, 1966). The child, thus, often remembers less than the adult. These claims do not depend upon a particular model of mental limitations (Olson, 1973). A shorter span of immediate memory in the child for instance may be explained either in terms of the child having a smaller number of mental 'slots', or in terms of the child failing to use an appropriate processing strategy, or in terms of both.

So far as linguistic performance is concerned, mental constraints are both short-term and long-term (Slobin, 1973). Short-term constraints involve the use of speech for comprehension and production; they are usually viewed in terms of memory and attention (Shallice, 1975). For instance, it has been shown that the length of a child's utterance is typically less than that of an adult (Brown, 1973). Also, when asked to imitate adult sentences, the child reduces the length to match its own spontaneous utterance. Long-term constraints involve the storage and organisation of the rule system for language. For example, the best predictor of the order of acquisition of some parts of language appears to be relative semantic complexity; the past tense '-ed', indicating only 'time' is learnt before the third person singular ending of the verb '-s', indicating both 'time' and 'number' (Brown); the use of 'big/small' to refer to any dimension, occurs before 'high/low' which refers to a single dimension (Clark, 1972). A further aspect of long-term memory is the manner of rule acquisition. An hypothesis-testing model of acquisition has been proposed, which selects rules according to their relative simplicity (Katz, 1966). An alternative possibility is a discovery-procedures model, which registers and accumulates properties of sentences (Braine, 1971).

The question arises as to whether there is a relationship between short-term and long-term limitations in mental capacity. Limitations in the processing of speech and in the organisation of linguistic rules may be independent. It has been argued, however, that the child is limited, in the complexity of the rule system it can store and use, by the same cognitive processes which limit the representation of information in short-term memory (Olson, 1973). A similar suggestion is that the form of linguistic rules is determined by short-term processing limitations, because the rules refer to a system which is embodied in the medium of rapidly-fading, temporally ordered sound and because they must be accessed and used during rapid speech processing. Some relation thus seems likely.

Mental capacity is also limited for the L2 learner. Indeed, if tasks involve more than the minimal linguistic complexity (Long and Harding-Esch, 1977); the limitations on internal processes are likely to be similar in most respects to those in L1 learning. The similarity is most obvious for those internal processes involved in the organisation and memory of verbal materials and least obvious for attention. The L2 learner, like the adult, is more able to direct his own attention and to allow his attention to be directed by others through the medium of words (J.S. Bruner, 1975). In general, the differences from the child relate to the greater cognitive and emotional maturity of the L2 learner.

In terms of short-term constraints, maturity seems to be of little help. Even advanced L2 learners fail to group in recall words belonging to the same semantic category (Cook, 1977) and omit important but not subsidiary information in the summary and recall of text (Long and Harding-Esch, 1977). In contrast, tasks with minimal linguistic requirements such as deductive reasoning (d'Anglejean et al, 1977) and the verification of order relations may be performed almost as well in a second language as in a first. In terms of long-term constraints associated with the storage and organisation of linguistic rules, L2 learning appears to have much in common with L1 learning. The order of acquisition of certain syntactic constructions, for

13

example 'easy to please' versus 'eager to please', may be the same in both (Cook, 1973). An important difference however, appears to be the conscious involvement of the L2 learner in the learning process as shown by spontaneous practice and active strategies of self-checking (Stern, 1975). Indeed, along with avoidance strategies (Schachter, 1974), a notion of the conscious monitoring of syntax has been proposed as perhaps *the* distinctive feature of L2 learning (Krashen, 1977).

There are at least three implications that can be drawn from this for the teaching of second languages. One is that teaching materials and techniques have to take into account the various forms of mental limitation. For example, the length of sentences that are presented to the learner should have some relationship to the span that the learner has for that kind of material. Another implication is that teaching should not neglect the re-development of linguistic strategies spontaneously used in the first language such as the clustering of vocabulary in memory, the interpretation of reference, and the making of inferences. The implication is that teaching might attempt to exploit rather more those specific features of L2 learning, such as avoidance and conscious monitoring of language, which may be only poorly developed in the use of the first language.

There are particular stages in language development through which all children progress, even if the rate of progression varies

It is still impossible to say how consistent children are in the order in which they acquire language, because of the limitations of the research. Nevertheless, consistent orders of acquisition have been found. The reasons for this may be certain universal strategies that L1 learners adopt for dealing with language, certain inherent characteristics of the language itself, the dependence of some aspects of language on cognition, or the frequency with which certain forms are heard and used. Hatch and others have argued that consistent orders of acquisition of language forms appear in children because the kinds of interaction the children engage in are necessarily limited. Partly there are a limited number of things to talk about, partly the interaction process itself requires certain types of language, and partly, adults share preconceptions of the child's linguistic abilities. First language development is probably the product not of any one of these factors, but of the interaction between them.

In the case of L2 learning, there have been several reports of research in which the order of acquisition of language items by learners of different mother tongues, different ages, in different situations, appears to be constant. Both Chinese- and Spanish-speaking children in America appeared to acquire certain English morphemes in the same order (Dulay and Burt, 1974) and this order correlated with that obtained with adults (Bailey, Madden and Krashen, 1974). Order of acquisition was the same for three groups of learners of different ages, but their rate of progress was different (Fathmann, 1975). In these, and other researches, the order of acquisition of morphemes was found to be slightly different from that found in L1 learning. In contrast, it has been found that various other syntactic processes (e.g. the difference between *easy to do* and *eager to do*, between *ask* and *promise* someone to do something, and relative clause formation) appear to be learnt in the same order as

14

in L1 (d'Anglejean and Tucker, 1975; Cook, 1973). But in general there is some difficulty in interpreting these and related results as there are several methodological problems (Rosansky, 1975; Cook, 1978; Schachter and Celce-Muria, 1977).

Nevertheless there has been a large amount of research of varying quality into the problem of the order of acquisition of language items in English as a second language and other languages, most of it supporting the idea of a constant order among learners. If this proves to be true, the most cautious implication for language teaching is that teaching sequences should be avoided that go counter to the order of acquisition that has been discovered. If the learner is going to pass through the same stages almost regardless of the order in which we present the language to him, we might as well accommodate our order of presentation to his order of acquisition. Rather than the kind of ordering that has been used so far, based either on some notion of linguistic complexity or some arbitrary division and sequencing of the target the learner is aiming at, we need grading and sequencing based on the actual progression of the learner; indeed some attempts have already been made to base order of acquisition on the errors that learners made.

The child learns to adapt its language use to particular situations

Much research has been directed at establishing how a child learns the grammar and functions of a first language (Brown, 1973). Only recently, however, has an attempt been made to find out how and when the child learns to adapt its language to particular situations (Berko-Gleason, 1973). The situations of concern here are primarily social and involve communication with different audiences, such as other children and adults.

Adult language is itself flexible. Formality of address between adults is an obvious example, in which factors such as relative social status, employment and income may all be influential (Ervin-Tripp, 1973). Further, adult speech addressed to children rather than to other adults tends to have simpler syntax, with few or no embedded or conjoined clauses, to be slower with different patterns of pausing, to use a restricted vocabulary and to contain few mistakes or ungrammatical turns of phrase (Farwell, 1973).

Research suggests the child acquires a similar — albeit initially crude — flexibility. Very small children, for example, babble to parents and siblings but not to strangers (Berko-Gleason, 1973). Likewise, whining — a repetitive, insistent sing-song demand or complaint — may be reserved for parents. Flexibility increases as children grow older. Reports indicate that children of four years and above modify their speech to younger children in contrast to peers or adults, by omitting verbs, and increasing one word utterances, repetitions and attention-getting words, such as the child's name and 'Look' (Gelman and Shatz, 1972). Elsewhere it has been shown that they address babies with short repetitive utterances, while they address children of their own age with sounds, but no endearments (Berko-Gleason). Children often address their youngers in the socialising code of the parents, indicating what should be done and how ('Don't run!'; 'You share them!'). Children may also treat strangers formally in terms of greetings and politeness (Bates, 1974). In general, although the flexibility of the child's speech code is very limited below the age of five years, there is a considerable increase by the age of ten.

At present there is little agreement about what determines the speed at which the child learns to adapt its language for others. Some suppose that taking another's perspective is incompatible with the basically ego-centric nature of the young child and must therefore await later development. Others suppose that making allowances for others requires some mental capacity and is possible at all stages of development for the child, providing its mental resources are not exceeded by competing demands (Krauss and Glucksberg, 1973).

There is even less research on the L2 learner's adaptation of language to particular situations than on the child's. However, since the audience in the classroom is largely restricted to the teacher and fellow learners, it is reasonable to assume that initially at least there is less encouragement for the L2 learner to acquire flexible language. Indeed, it might be argued that the often formal nature of the classroom interactions produces an essentially inflexible language, which only considerable exposure to the target language culture is able to break down. Even when modified by long exposure, the resultant 'informal' language may not itself be much more flexible. Even advanced learners tend to import informal expressions into tasks in which they are not appropriate — for example in the summary and recall of a speech made at the European Parliament (Long and Harding-Esch, 1977).

Once in the second language culture, the learner's flexibility might be expected to improve. Firstly, the types of different audience are likely to increase, including both native and non-native speakers but of a different language. Secondly, the learner is likely to possess considerable flexibility in a first language which may transfer to a second as linguistic proficiency increases. Not all types of adaptation, however, should be interpreted in terms of code-switching flexibility. Pressure to communicate with native target language speakers may lead to avoidance strategies by which complex syntactic forms are not used (Schachter, 1974) or to simple language systems (pidgins) (Schumann, 1975). Neither necessarily involves sensitivity to different social situations. Speaking with less proficient non-native speakers with a different first language, however, might be expected to elicit those typical strategies of foreigner talk to be discussed below.

One implication for second language teaching is that, as the learner becomes more proficient, he should be encouraged to transfer the knowledge already possessed concerning the need for situational flexibility to the second language, through techniques such as role-playing. In addition the learner should be made aware of the possibility for being flexible even at early stages of language acquisition through such processes as simplification. In general, except at an advanced level, the classroom has treated language as unvarying and has not encouraged the learner to appreciate the varieties of language that make up the native speaker's communicative competence. The classroom needs to present a greater variety of language so that the learner's flexibility can be developed, rather than a single variety of classroom language.

Adults adapt their speech in systematic ways when talking to children

The characteristics of speech addressed to children by mothers and others, including older children, has been divided into elements of simplification and clarification (Sachs and Devin, 1976). Simplification strategies include: shorter mean length of utterance; restriction of tenses; restriction of number of elements before the verb; less subordination. Clarification strategies include: naming, repetition (mother repeating herself and repeating child's words); frequent questions; frequent imperatives; exaggerated intonation. A small proportion of 'motherese', as it is now often called, appears to include linguistic guidance (eg recasting sentences).

While it is reasonably clear that people do modify their language when speaking to young children, it is not obvious what role this plays in the child's acquisition process. It might be a necessary part of the process, but so far no reports have been able to contrast language learning situations where motherese occurs with those where it doesn't. Presumably this type of language modification is a product of the mothers' conception of communication strategies and is quite strongly determined by what the children can or wish to say. However, there is no evidence that children use mothers as a L2 learner might use a teacher or native speaker (eg for explanations of language structure) except to ask for names. Some children's learning strategies and their mothers' interaction patterns may be mismatched, thus causing learning to be delayed (Nelson, 1973). If motherese was clear, it might be evidence for refuting the transformationalists' claim that the language children were exposed to was too deformed to be usable as data for grammar construction by a child who was not equipped with innate knowledge of language structure. The evidence is, however, not conclusive.

It is not clear how far clarification strategies have reinforcing effects. Indications of partial success in communication may reward the child but evidence to support this is scarce. The utility of viewing motherese as analogous to school instruction seems rather small, as there is as yet no evidence showing the lasting effects of these strategies on the language product.

In relating this statement to the L2 situation, the 'adult' 'translates' as the native speaker or teacher, and the 'child', as the learner. Outside the classroom, native speakers do use 'foreigner talk', that is to say, adapt their speech in systematic ways when talking to foreign learners, and compensate for the learner's poor expression by using many strategies for maintaining the conversation and for eliciting the meaning the non-native speaker is trying to express. Popularly, both adopt the strategy of talking loudly and slowly, but there are many more subtle strategies of repair of lost contact, repetition of key words, simplification of syntax, and use of words that are believed international such as 'savvy', many of which seem similar to those used by adults to children (Ferguson, 1975; Hatch). It is not clear however whether foreigner talk is something that native speakers believe they do rather than actually do; an experiment in which a foreigner asked natives for directions did not reveal much use of foreigner talk (Stocker-Edel, 1977). Whether these alleged foreigner talk strategies are really analagous to the verbal strategies used when speaking to children is not certain — and neither is their role in the learner's developing competence. In the classroom, while teachers typically control their use of the language to relate it to the level of attainment of their pupils, frequently principles of teaching methods are used to govern this control, such as requiring only 'full' sentences or grammatically accurate ones.

As with the previous statement, the implication is that the classroom needs to present a greater variety of language and to use techniques in which pupils and teachers adopt a variety of roles. For example, if the pupils are never allowed to initiate questions or give orders in the second language, they cannot be expected to learn to do so. Also, if it is true that L2 learners profit from conversational interaction as L1 learners do, then a way needs to be found of bringing opportunities for such interactions into the classroom. As always this should be qualified with the reminder that at present we still need to find out exactly what types of interaction already take place in language classrooms before we can advocate particular changes (Fauselow, 1977). While this implication is speculative, it can hardly be denied that the principles of simplification that have governed the choice of classroom language have little connection with the principles underlying foreigner talk or motherese; if these simplified varieties play a part in the learning process, then classroom language will have to move in the direction of these simplified forms that are sometimes addressed to learners.

To conclude this paper, it is evident that the vital question the teacher must decide is the extent to which he should modify the classroom situation to be more like that found in 'natural' language learning. If he believes that L2 learning in a classroom is entirely different from language learning outside a classroom, we will feel no need to modify the classroom in this way. If, however, he believes that language learning is language learning wherever it occurs, as we would claim the evidence suggests, then he will have to bring many features of 'natural' learning into the classroom, always bearing in mind that some of them may not permit transfer. Some of these features have been mentioned during the argument. Perhaps to sum up it might be said that the classroom that takes them into account is likely to be a freer, more spontaneous, place with less direction by the teacher and less control of the language but at the same time provide a greater wealth of activities and interactions.

As a postscript to this paper we should like to take up briefly the point that was made earlier about the lack of evidence on certain crucial issues and suggest some further research that is necessary before very concrete suggestions can be made for a teaching methodology based on a knowledge of second language learning. At the moment we do have several studies of the learner's language in terms of syntactic development and error analysis. We do, however, need not only studies of other languages being learnt but also much greater work on the development of other aspects of language — semantics, phonology, language functions, and so on. This work should not only describe what occurs but should also attempt to explain it by postulating processes and strategies in the learner that cause the various phenomena of second language learning. Another point that needs clarification is the relationship between language learning and other mental processes, such as the development of memory span and its relationship to language learning, the contribution of language

18

to the various stages of conceptual development and vice versa, the effects of learning a second language on the individual, whether beneficial or harmful. Furthermore, we do not have sufficient information at present on the learner's situation, not just in physical or general terms but also in terms of the specific social interactions that take place in 'natural' learning situations and in the classroom. Lastly because of the variety of mother tongues that pupils speak in British schools today we need to know more both about the utility of preserving and encouraging the mother tongue within the educational setting in Britain and about the peculiarities of teaching a language such as French through the medium of a language that is not itself the pupils' mother tongue. Ultimately this should lead to a coherent theory of second language learning, rather than the heterogenous assortment of ideas that we have today.

References

d'Anglejean, A.; Gagnon, N.; Tucker, G.R.; and Winsberg, S. *Solving problems in deductive reasoning; the performance of adult second language learners.* Paper presented to the 8th Conference on Applied Linguistics, University of Michigan, 1977.

d'Anglejean, A.; and Tucker, G. R. 'The acquisition of complex English structures by adult learners.' *Language Learning*, 25, 2, 1975, pp 281–296.

Bailey, N.; Madden, C.; and Krashen, S.D. 'Is there a "natural sequence" in adult second language learning?' *Language Learning*, 24, 2, 1974, pp 235–243.

Bates, E. 'Acquisition of pragmatic competence.' *Journal of Child Language*, 1, 2, 1974, pp 277–281.

Berko Gleason, J. 'Code-switching in children's language.' In *Cognitive development and the acquisition of language.* Edited by T.E. Moore. Academic Press, New York, 1973, pp 159–167.

Bousfield, W.A.; Esterson, J.; and Whitmarsh, G.A. 'A study of developmental changes in conceptual and perceptual associative clustering.' *Journal of Genetic Psychology*, 92, 1958, pp 95–102.

Braine, M.D.S. 'On two types of models of the internalization of grammars.' In *The ontogenesis of grammar.* Edited by D.I. Slobin. New York: Academic Press, 1941, pp 153–186.

Braine, M.D.S. 'Children's first word combinations.' *Monographs of the Society for Research in Child Development*, 164, 1976.

Brown, R.W. *A first language: the early stages* Allan & Unwin, 1973.

Bruner, J.S. 'The ontogenesis of speech acts,' *Journal of Child Language*, 2, 1, 1975, pp 1–19.

Bruner, J.S. 'Language as an instrument of thought.' *Problems of language and learning.* Edited by A. Davies. Heinemann, 1975, pp 61–88.

Clark, E.V. 'On the child's acquisition of antonyms in two semantic fields.' *Journal of Verbal Learning and Verbal Behavior*, 11, 1972, pp 750–758.

Clark, E.V. 'What's in a word? On the child's acquisition of semantics in his first language.' In *Cognitive development and the acquisition of language.* Edited by T.E. Moore. Academic Press, 1973, pp 65–110.

Cook, V.J. 'The comparison of language development in native children and foreign adults.' *IRAL*, XI/1, 1973, pp 13–28.

Cook, V.J. 'Cognitive processes in second language learning.' *IRAL*, XV/1, 1977, pp 1–20.

Cook, V.J. 'Second language learning: a psycholinguistic perspective.' *Language Teaching and Linguistics: Abstracts*, 11–2, 1978, pp 73–89.

Corder, S.P. 'The significance of learner's errors.' *IRAL*, V/4, 1967, pp 161–170.

Cromer, R. 'The development of language and cognition: the cognition hypothesis.' In *New perspectives in child development*. Edited by B. Foss. Penguin, 1974.

Dulay, H.; and Burt, M. 'A new perspective on the creative construction process in child second language acquisition.' *Language Learning*, 24, 2, 1974, pp 253–278.

Ervin-Tripp, S.M. 'The structure of communicative choice.' In *Language acquisition and communicative choice*. Edited by A.S. Dil. Stanford University Press, 1973, pp 302–373.

Fanselow, J.F. 'Beyond Rashomon—conceptualizing and describing the teaching act.' *TESOL Quarterly*, 11, 1, 1977, pp 17–39.

Farwell, C.B. 'The language spoken to children.' *Papers and Reports on Child Development*, Stanford University, 5, 1973, pp 31–62.

Fathmann, A. 'The relationship between age and second language productive ability.' *Language Learning*, 25, 2, 1975, pp 245–253.

Ferguson, C.A. 'Toward a characterization of English foreigner talk.' *Anthropological Linguistics*, 17, 1, 1975, pp 1–14.

Flavell, J.H.; Beach, D.R.; and Chinsky, J.M. 'Spontaneous verbal rehearsal in a memory task as a function of age.' *Child Development*, 37, 2, 1966.

Gardner, R.C.; Smythe, P.C.; Clément, R.; and Gliksman, L. 'Second-language learning: a social psychological perspective.' *Canadian Modern Language Review*, 32/3, 1976, pp 198–213.

Gelman, R.; and Shatz, M. 'Listener-dependent adjustments in the speech of four-year-olds.' Paper presented at the Psychonomic Society Meeting, St Louis, Missouri, 1972.

Hagen, J.W. 'Some thoughts on how children learn to remember.' *Human Development*, 14, 1971, pp 262–271.

Halliday, M.A.K. *Learning how to mean: explorations in the development of language*. Edward Arnold, 1975.

Hatch, E.M. 'Discourse analysis and second language acquisition: a book of readings.' In *Second language acquisition*. Edited by E. Hatch. Newbury House, 1978, pp 401–435.

Kagan, J.; and Lewis, M. 'Studies of attention in the human infant.' *Merrill-Palmer Quarterly*, 11, 1965, pp 404–425.

Katz, J.J. *The philosophy of language*. Harper & Row, 1966.

Keenan, E.O. 'Conversational competence in children.' *Journal of Child Language*, 1, 2, 1974, pp 163–183.

Krashen, S.T. 'Formal and informal linguistic environments in language acquisition and language learning.' *TESOL Quarterly*, 10, 2, 1976, pp 157–168.

Krashen, S.D. 'The monitor model for adult second language performance.' In

Viewpoints on English as a second language. Edited by M. Burt, H. Dulay and M. Finocchario. Regents, 1977, pp 152–161.

Krauss R.M.; and Glucksberg. S. 'Social and non-social speech.' *Scientific American*, February, 1974.

Long, J.B.; and Harding-Esch, E. 'Summary and recall of text in first and second languages: some factors contributing to performance differences.' In *Proceedings of the Nato symposium on language interpretation and communication.* Edited by H.W. Sinaiko and D. Gerver. Plenum Press, 1977.

Long, J.B.; and Harding-Esch, E. *Effects of task difficulty on recall performance in first and second languages* (in preparation).

Macmanara, J. 'Comparison between first and second language learning.' *Die Neueren Sprachen*, 1976, pp 175–188.

Mclaughlin, B. 'Second language learning in children.' *Psychological Bulletin*, 84, 3, 1973, pp 438–459.

Nelson, K. 'Structure and strategy in learning to talk.' *Monographs of the Society for Research in Child Development.* 149, 1973.

Nemser, W. 'Approximative systems of foreign language learners.' *IRAL*, IX/2, 1971, pp 115–123.

Olson, G.M. 'Developmental changes in memory and the acquisition of language.' In *Cognitive development and the acquisition of language.* Edited by T.E. Moore. Academic Press, 1973, pp 145–157.

Padilla, A.M. 'Acquisition of fourteen grammatical morphemes in the speech of bilingual children.' Mimeo, UCLA (in preparation).

Rosansky, E. 'The critical period for the acquisition of language: some cognitive developmental considerations.' *Working Papers in Bilingualism*, 6, 1975, pp 92–102.

Rosansky, E. 'Methods and morphemes in second language acquisition research.' *Language Learning*, 26, 2, 1976, pp 409–425.

Rutherford, R.W.; Freeth, M.E.A.; and Mercer, E.S. 'Topics of conversation in the speech of fifteen-year-old children.' *Nuffield Foreign Languages Teaching Materials Project Occasional Paper No. 44*, 1970.

Sachs, J.; and Devin, J. 'Young children's use of age-appropriate speech styles in social interaction and role-playing.' *Journal of Child Language*, 3, 1, 1976, pp 81–98.

Schachter, J. 'An error in error analysis.' *Language Learning*, 24, 2, 1974, pp 205–214.

Schachter, J.; and Celce-Muria, M. 'Some reservations concerning error analysis.' *TESOL Quarterly*, 11, 4, 1977, pp 441–451.

Schumann, J. 'Implications of pidginisation and creolisation for the study of adult second language acquisition.' In *New frontiers in second language learning.* Edited by J.H. Schumann and N. Stenson. Newbury House, 1975.

Selinker, L. 'Interlanguage.' *IRAL*, 10/3, 1972, pp 209–231.

Shallice, T. 'On the contents of primary memory.' In *Attention and performance V.* Edited by P.M.A. Rabbitt and S. Dornic. Academic Press, 1975.

Sinclair, H. 'Developmental psycholinguistics.' In *Studies in cognitive development: essays in honor of Jean Piaget.* Edited by D. Elkind and J.H. Flavell. Oxford University Press, 1969.

Sinclair, H. 'Sensorimotor action patterns as a condition for the acquisition of syntax.' In *Language acquisition: models and methods*. Edited by R. Huxley and E. Ingram. Academic Press, 1971, pp 121–135.

Slobin, D.I. 'Cognitive prerequisites for the development of grammar'. In *Studies of child language development*. Edited by C.A. Ferguson and D.I. Slobin. Holt Rinehart & Winston, 1973.

Smith, N.V. *The acquisition of phonology: a case study*. Cambridge University Press, 1973, pp 175–209.

Stern, H.H. 'What can we learn from the good language learner?' *Canadian Modern Language Review*, 31/4, 1975, pp 304–318.

Stocker-Edel, A. 'The responses of Wellingtonians to a foreigner's English.' *Archivum Linguisticum*, VIII, 1977, pp 13–27.

Tremaine, R.V. 'Piagetian equilibration processes in syntax learning.' In *Developmental psycholinguistics: theory and applications*. Edited by D.P. Dato. Georgetown University Press, Washington DC, 1975, pp 255–265.

Trim, J.L.M. 'A unit/credit scheme for adult language learning.' In CILT Reports and Papers 11: *Teaching languages to adults for special purposes*, CILT, 1974.

Valdmann, A. 'Error analysis and pedagogical ordering: the determination of pedagogically motivated sequences.' In *Some implications of linguistic theory for applied linguistics*. Edited by S.P. Corder and E. Roulet. Association Internationale pour la recherche et la diffusion des méthodes audio-visuelles et structuro-globales, Brussels, 1975, pp 105–126.

2. English as a mother tongue

Harold Rosen and
Leslie Stratta

An historical perspective

Hundreds of thousands of teachers and their pupils are engaged at every stage of our school system in a set of activities which we have come to call 'English'. What they will be doing can scarcely be understood by using a simple cause-effect model. The force of history can be detected in much of it, expressing itself in traditional practices, conventions and even rituals. Other forces at work in contemporary society will push teachers this way or that. Direct intervention by the examination system, inspectors and local authority fiat (and these interventions themselves need explaining) will sometimes be decisive. While it may be true, as Mulcaster asserted in 1582, that 'necessity itself doth call for English' there have been doubters ever since. They have argued either that the curriculum as a whole should be left through its oblique functioning to produce the necessary competences or, in a more patrician context, that no-one needs teaching his mother tongue. The force of these arguments has often pushed the defenders of the subject to cast around for matter which is beyond all cavil distinctively their own, be it grammar or literature. The Newbolt Report of 1921, *The teaching of English in England*, deployed its rhetoric to plead for the central importance of the subject and used its evidence to display at what a low level it was functioning in English shcools.

A century of theoretical discussion and analysis and a century of mass education have been marked by the constant reiteration of certain viewpoints (some of them bitterly opposed to each other), clearly articulated bafflement about the boundaries of the subject and the infusion at certain critical moments of new claims and new proposals with a millennial ring to them. Confronted by a list of activities, which might at this moment be found on offer in our schools under the banner of English, anyone might reasonably conclude that the legacy we have come into is a trunk-load of items so heterogeneous, so random, so irreconcilable that no pattern can be rescued from them (traditional grammatical parsing and clause analysis, improvised drama, thematic work, creative writing, comprehension exercises, the remnants of rhetoric, media studies, film-making, 'set books', the learning and teaching of English as a second language, practical English, commercial English, English in humanities, etc).

It is possible to trace, then, repeated attempts to answer the questions: 'English for what?' and 'What should pupils be doing in English lessons?' But there is another difficulty. If we examine the considerable literature which has attempted to answer these questions, we are obliged to ask ourselves to what extent the explication of fresh aims, the clarion calls and the polemic are in any way a reliable indication of what was happening in classrooms or to what extent they changed in any fundamental way what subsequently happened in classrooms. The results of the survey conducted by the Bullock Committee show very clearly the huge difference between the prevailing philosphy of those who get into print and what most teachers do. This is not to argue that there have not been powerful and influential voices, but only that many (often the majority) of teachers have also listened to other voices like those which speak through the imperatives of examination syllabi and textbooks. What teachers of English do cannot be simply a matter of their own personal commitments or whims.

Thus it is possible to find wide divergences from school to school: English being taught in ways which have changed little in a half-century or in ways which seem to some outrageously *avant-garde*. These divergences are the more likely in a period of questioning about the curriculum and even more likely in English since, given the least encouragement, it will reach out beyond itself to everything in human experience. In that sense English is not ultimately about itself but for those developing greater competence in its use. That being so, it is not surprising that in a period of relative freedom, some teachers took it wherever it led. Nevertheless, there is a broad band of practice or at least shared attitudes, however implicit, which emerges from the diversity. The Bullock Report (1975) commenting on diversity and some widespread notions about it, had this to say:

> Generalisations are commonly made to the effect that one or another set of attitudes has virtually swept the board (p.4) It would be absurdly oversimplifying to say that English teaching has, without light or shade, separated itself into factions . . .(p.5)

The quest for English is also made more difficult by the ease with which the same label can be attached to kinds of work which in the classroom emerge as very different experiences. Thus 'the discussion method' can turn out to be anything from the most formal and constrained exchanges between a teacher and a whole class, or small groups apparently gossiping in much the same way as they would out of school.

This is by no means a question of the good teacher against the bad but how in the absence of clear principles, the rallying-cries can be made to mean almost anthing. 'Creativity' has been just such a rallying-cry. It is also a feature of present-day English teaching that teachers are probably much more confident about what they are rejecting than they are about the alternatives to them. This is scarcely surprising and must apply to all attempts at serious innovation. So we may say with confidence that large numbers of teachers have rejected for ever the kinds of drills and 'exercises' which have been the staple of hundreds of textbooks and the dreary routines which turned the study of literature into the memorising of plots and the hunt for examples of literary devices. On the other hand, few of the same teachers would be nearly so confident in attempting to devise a programme to create confident speakers and writers or to describe how literature should play a central role in the development of their pupils.

In the generalities offered so far two huge and related factors affecting present-day practice have not been mentioned. The first is that the raising of the school-leaving age and the coming of the comprehensive school have obliged us to ask in a form much more compelling than in the past 'What kind of English teaching is right for everyone?'. In our secondary schools, especially those in the great conurbations, it has become clear that programmes, whatever their merits, which were built on the assumption of unquestioning acceptance, or at least tolerance, could no longer succeed. Much of the desperate innovation which is such an easy target for mockery, looks very different in a context where everything the teacher does has to win acceptance from alienated sceptical pupils who have often remained untouched by most of what school has offered them. They know now that the chief rewards of the school system are not for them, that their own language, however powerful it may be for their present purposes, seems of little value within school. It is this, perhaps more than anything else, which has led teachers themselves to turn a critical eye on concepts of English teaching which had hitherto gone unchallenged. Thus from some came the accusation that English had been centrally concerned with the inculcation of middle-class values with a bogus common culture (bogus because it was a miserable diluted version of an élitist high culture), with contempt for and ignorance of popular culture, with a deliberate oppression of the pupils' own language, with a domestication process, realised through language, designed to meet the needs of the labour market. From others there came an intensification of the old demand that English should 'prepare pupils for society' by concentrating on practical day-to-day uses of language; English could also be swallowed up in communicating the specific needs of employers. Whereas the sixties had seemed hospitable to innovation, the late seventies have brought a change in the climate and the government itself has put its weight behind the 'back-to-basics' demand, though how far back and to what particular basics is far from clear.

The other factor, which very late in the day is moving to the centre of attention, is that whereas we could, with some superficial credibility, behave as though in our schools we were dealing with an homogeneous linguistic community, this is now manifestly untrue. Our schools contain some pupils whose English is still an 'inter-language' between a language other than English and a target language the nature of which is still not agreed (is the target the regional vernacular, a new English dialect, standard-with-RP?); we have pupils who are bilingual and plurilingual being taught by teachers who have not been trained to understand the implications; we have pupils who speak an overseas dialect of English or whose speech is influenced by it; we have pupils who can switch into a creole even though they were not brought up to speak it. Faced by this linguistic diversity, about which very little is known, English programmes of almost any kind have a need to reckon with new complexities. What is the status of the first language in the pupil's own eyes, in the eyes of fellow pupils, his own parents, his teachers? In other words, what difference does it make if your first language is Italian or a Caribbean creole or Cantonese?

The languages and dialects of these pupils are at one and the same time the channel for their own unique cultures and part of those cultures. How does the old call for schools to be the promoters of a common culture sound in this new context? What looked like a liberal humanist aim can easily become its opposite, an excuse for ignoring or even oppressing cultural minorities, declaring that the entrance money to the English Language Club must be paid by deserting their own cultures or keeping them discreetly out of sight in school hours. In fact, the glaring linguistic diversity in our schools can be seen as bringing into sharp focus the way in which within English teaching we have dealt with linguistic diversity in the past. If schools have in general

25

not accommodated, much less cherished, the cultural identity of millions of pupils, they have done so partly at least by making them lose confidence in their own code through which their deepest feelings and understandings have been nourished.

English now stands at the confluence of two distinct traditions each of which has left its mark. It is worth remembering that it is in any case very much of a Johnny-come-lately amidst the established figures of our curriculum. In the universities and the public schools, it was openly sneered at, a mere soft option alternative to the classics for women and weak students or it gained entry by turning itself into philology and Anglo-Saxon, leaving its students better informed about the great vowel shift and *Beowulf* than they were about contemporary English or *The Prelude*. As a lately-arrived second-class citizen it could only servilely ape its betters and attempt to put on all the prestigious robes of classical scholarship. At school level it meant the adoption of the time-honoured practices which had accreted around the learning of Latin and Greek, for most a drudgery without meaning. The same practices installed themselves in the grammar schools where, it has often been remarked, English was treated not only as though it were a dead language, but also a foreign one. It is possible to put side-by-side a school edition of say Milton's *Paradise Lost* and Virgil's *Aeneid* and to see no difference between the 'apparatus' in which the texts are embedded. It was, for example, a straight transfer from Latin teaching which took *oratio obliqua* and *oratio recta* into English text-book exercises which required a pupil to change passages from direct to indirect speech or vice versa.

School English also drew on another venerable source — classical rhetoric. In its day a vigorous field of scholarship setting itself the task of examining what made a discourse effective, it degenerated as it accumulated its categories and items, and from being a study of discourse it became a pedagogical method; it was assumed, as it has been assumed so often since, that if you know what means accepted writers have used, can define them and identify them, you become a better writer. The borrowings from rhetoric were probably inspired by the never-ending search for content to put backbone and difficulty into the subject. Thus the preoccupation with figures of speech and devices of style, which as loss of confidence grew in the efficacy of the study, dwindled from a huge catalogue to metaphor and simile. The final ingredient was supplied by supposedly authoritative publications like Fowler's *The King's English* designed to guide the nervous through the thickets of acceptable usage and to diagnose stylistic diseases to be guarded against, thus Johnsonese, journalese, verbosity, genteel variations, Malapropism. Fowler was plundered for notes, text book exercises and above all examination questions. Small wonder then if English teaching in the old secondary system appeared to be an arbitrary mixture unified only by a concept of English which had little to do with real people using and responding to language in effective and important ways.

The secondary modern schools and later, the comprehensives, might in theory have struck out on their own for an English more suited to their needs, but overwhelmingly this is not what happened at first. For those of their pupils for whom examinations passes at sixteen plus seemed a realisable goal they took over from the grammar school its form of teaching English just as they took over its external symbols of prestige, uniforms, speech days, prefect systems etc. But the comprehensives were the inheritors of another tradition, an unbroken line; dame school, Church school, Board school, elementary school. From the 1870 Act onwards the education of all children became a national commitment and the elementary school became a permanent feature of the urban landscape. It was conceived at the outset as an institution with very fixed limitations — minimal literacy and numeracy needed by a rapidly expanding industrial society plus the inculcation of suitable moral virtues, obedience, cleanliness and punctuality. Indeed, anxieties were repeatedly expressed that anything beyond a carefully constrained minimum would give working-class children ideas beyond their station. The Cockerton Judgement was the legal expression of a determination to prevent them from learning more than had been laid down as the minimum. In that setting there was nothing which was even called English on the timetable of elementary schools and when it did come in it was used only to mean parsing and sentence analysis. For the rest there were separate timetabled periods for composition, reading, spelling, dictation etc.

These two traditions, that of the selective system and that of mass education are what merge today in our schools. It is an uneasy embrace but it accounts in part for the persistence of ideas and procedures which seem ill-assorted if not actually obsolete, ways of presenting literature, isolated exercising of bits of language (antonyms and synonyms etc), a syllabus with no central informing principle, remedial classes with a down-to-earth, no-nonsense approach to literacy. But from the very beginning there have been other voices and, indeed, here too there has been at least one unbroken tradition from Matthew Arnold through the Newbolt Report, George Sampson, Caldwell Cook and Leavis. In their quite distinct ways what they have shared is an insistence that English should stand at the heart of the curriculum, that literature should stand at the heart of English teaching, that the experience of learning English should be a humanising experience. For them, English was essentially a literary culture embattled *against* the prevailing social forces of its day. It would come as a shock to many today that a government report could state boldly that:

> There is the delusion, still sometimes surviving, that the only education which they (the people) ought to have is that which trains their hands to the plough or their eyes to the needle, which has exclusively in view the making of miners, or factory girls, engineers, or cooks. That is the educational "lie in the soul", whether it comes from the selfishness of those who wish to employ, or the shortsightedness of those who wish for employment. The whole of our Report is a protest against it. (Newbolt p.61)

Yet this vein of thinking could run in different directions — into distaste for all changes in contemporary society, into the teaching of English as a training against commercial culture (discrimination is the watchword), into messianic hopes that English could destroy class barriers, into the belief that a few highly trained sensibilities could keep alive the best culture. It is remarkable that out of the same tradition come two opposing standpoints, élitist and populist, the one urging different programmes for different social classes, the other a vital and compelling programme which could be fitting for all children without surrendering humanist ideals.

The discussion so far would not enable anyone to deduce what exactly they would be likely to find going on in the classroom of any teacher who espoused some of the approaches we have glanced at. The reason is not far to seek; it is that, in spite of repeated efforts to make it so, English cannot be a subject which is centrally concerned to transmit to pupils a coherent set of concepts, nor an essential body of information (supplying answers to questions like, 'What are the uses of the comma?', 'When was Milton born?'; 'What are the differences between loose and periodic sentences?', 'What is the origin of the words causeway, boycott, humour?'). It may well include such possibilities and others like them, but cannot be *centrally* concerned with them for we know that it is possible to be a highly competent, or even talented, user of the English language without knowing any of these things and conversely that those who know most about such things are very rarely the most elegant or exciting users of English. The whole history of the teaching of English has been bedevilled by attempts to give it a content which resembles that of other subjects in the curriculum (though they too have been having their crises of content). In a similar way efforts to impose certain kinds of sequential models have failed. Begin by writing sentences, then paragraphs, then 'essays'.

Nevertheless if we move to a certain level of generality it is easy enough to achieve near unanimity about the chief goals of English teaching, namely to create confident, capable users and receivers of spoken and written English. It is likely that most teachers would go even further and subscribe to the Bullock Report's declaration, 'We believe that language competence grows incrementally, through an interaction of writing, talk, reading and experience, the body of resulting work forming an organic whole.' Fewer would give assent to the preceding sentence, 'So we are not suggesting that the answer to improve standards is to be found in some such simple formula as: more grammar exercises, more formal speech training, more comprehension extracts'.

If English is to be 'an organic whole' and is, moreover, to be intimately related to experience rather than to be built on carefully prescribed curricula, then inevitably, though principles remain intact, the particular ways they are put into operation will depend on the lives and circumstances of a given class or group of pupils. The alternative to universal prescriptions becomes well-documented presentations of practice and collaborative activities of teachers forging their own policies and sharing their insights, discoveries and materials. No kit or scheme or text-book can do this for them.

To agree that all children should be made into effective readers, taking to literature with zest, able to grapple with discursive prose and well-equipped to detect manipulation through the written word, is not to agree about *how* this should be achieved. It is not the broad aims which divide teachers. It is their practice which shows them to be divided in their assumptions about how children gain mastery over their mother tongue. Here it is possible to detect the sharpest division broadly between those who believe that the use of language can be segmented into separate skills and each of these skills exercised separately, and those who believe that only the motivated use of language for real and worthwhile purposes can make a significant difference in language development. There are very important underlying issues here taking us into irreconcilable views about the nature of human beings.

The old view that the more you know about your language the better you would use it, still retains its hold even in its narrowest form — a knowledge of your language is chiefly 'knowing grammar', the same grammar as was taught 50 years ago. That view is, nevertheless, widely discredited and the teaching of grammar has been jettisoned by many schools and this has been legitimised by its disappearance.

There are two activities which make their way into English classrooms which highlight all we have already said, in particular the difficulty of making coherent the diversity of practice. Firstly, the study of language in general and the English language in particular continues to find some uneasy place, and secondly drama (as distinct from the literary study of dramatic texts) has won greater and greater acceptance. Let us look at them separately.

The loss of faith in the traditional methods of grammar teaching left behind it a vacuum. There has been a strong sense that if old-style grammar did nothing or very little to help mature speakers to use their mother tongue, then pupils had at the very least the right to know something about English just as they had the right to know something of their history. It seems clear that we are now at the stage when this demand is being realised in schemes which are based on modern ideas about language. There is much still to be resolved but the coming decade is likely to see the study of language firmly back in the curriculum but in a form very different from parsing and clause analysis. This segment of the English curriculum will stand out as the only one which resembles other traditional school subjects insofar as it will involve the understanding of certain basic concepts and the following of a programme which can be set out in advance in some detail.

Drama on the other hand stands at the opposite pole, some of its most powerful advocates arguing that only historical accident has left it under the aegis of English. Indeed, some suggest that it has more in common with music and art. In some schools a separate department or specialist has removed drama completely from its old home. Yet many English teachers feel that to abandon drama (with or without a text) is to lose a major form of the expressive and artistic use of language, that the dramatic mode is one means for exploring ideas and feelings and that only dramatic activity can bring dramatic texts to life. Dramatic language can be seen as a continuum beginning in spontaneous dialogue and ending with a polished stage performance.

Thus even when the centre of English teaching is clearly perceived, there jostle round its edges candidates for entry or exclusion. Debate rages about how they can be integrated into one subject or whether perhaps English ought legitimately to be regarded as several subjects.

English teaching today: strands, theory and practice

Strands in the teaching of English

Is it possible then to unlay some discernible strands in the teaching of English from what may appear to be the product of a set of historical accidents yoked as if by violence together? We have already said that from out of this plethora of seemingly contradictory activities there is a broad band of practice, or at least shared attitudes, however implicit, and that one of the chief goals of English teaching is to create confident, capable users and receivers of spoken and written English. But is it possible to flesh out these bare-boned statements into something which seems to have more coherence, and which one might confidently say constitutes the teaching of English in our secondary schools today? Well, yes and no. Yes, because there are some strands, which we have already hinted at. No, because there is no agreed curriculum, and what measure of agreement there is, is more the product of the demands of the external examination system, than agreement among teachers of English. For the rest of this paper the best we can do will be to unravel some different but important strands which we have discerned in the subject, and also to say something about new theories and practices which are informing the teaching of some of the more innovatory teachers.

As we examine the different strands, we cannot confidently say which, if any, is the most widespread. Despite the broad band of agreement about aims, individual teachers will choose to focus on those aspects of the subject which they consider important. As we have already said, all teachers of English are to some extent eclectic, although many will eschew some aspects. Some see themselves primarily as teachers of literature, others as teachers concerned with personal experience, others as teachers of language, but none, we suspect, see themselves as only this, not least because there are significant overlaps between several of the strands, none being so complete in itself as to exclude others.

We would not want to claim that the teaching of English at present is uniformly good. There have been significant advances in the subject in the past few years, which through ignorance have either been misunderstood, or ignored. What we can confidently say, however, is that a great deal of incisive thinking has gone on, and that some of it is being translated into imaginative classroom practice. Perhaps a discerning appraisal and selection from all of the following could do much to enhance the teaching of the subject.

Literature at the centre

For many teachers of English, literature is the central concern. The unbroken tradition from Arnold to Leavis and beyond, which we have already spoken about, has placed literature at the heart of English teaching as a humanising and civilising force, waging an unceasing battle against the Philistine forces of our modern society. For many of these teachers the Philistine forces, although perhaps taking on different guises from those of Arnold, are still as insidious, and ultimately destructive. For them the teaching of English is as much a bulwark against, as a preparation for, life in our modern society.

However, alongside this humanising thrust are other arguments for the centrality of literature. Literature, it is argued, is one of the most highly wrought art forms, and as such is worthy of study in its own right. By means of art the writer, arresting the untidy ebb and flow of day to day living, gives shape and order to life, and thereby offers the reader complex representations of the human condition for consideration and reflective contemplation. It is a means whereby an individual's experience can be imaginatively extended and his sympathies enlarged, a means whereby one man can, in a sense, become many men. Through the exploration of other visions of life, the teaching of literature can open up new horizons for the pupil, being concerned, as Lionel Trilling puts it, 'with the fullest and most precise account of variousness, possibility, complexity and difficulty.' Furthermore, as our culture has a long, rich and varied literary heritage, these teachers argue that they have an obligation to introduce their pupils to some aspects of it. Moreover, as their training has been concerned with acquiring the critical apparatus by which to study this literature, they have an important expertise to pass on to succeeding generations. Interestingly though, this concern for our heritage has led to a belief that there is a particular canon of works suitable for all pupils to study, and this coupled with the humanising thrust sometimes results in a culture-as-given approach, with its élitist overtones, and an ignoring of the culture of the pupil.

The belief in the centrality of literature has also led some teachers into a kind of ostrich-like position towards recent attitudes to language. Indeed there is a suspicion of anything called 'language' and open hostility to linguistics, as though to speak of English teaching in these terms is an act of betrayal. This has led to quite passionate arguments that the teacher does not really need to take 'language' very seriously, for within literature, which in some miraculous way always functions on all four cylinders, one can find answers to any language questions which might arise. Some who started in this tradition shed the élitist component without regret, but carried the critical awareness and sensibility into new fields – children's literature, neglected or unexplored works which spoke powerfully to their pupils, and even into the spoken word and the oral tradition. They were quick to share with their pupils any language used with power wherever they found it.

They were able to do this most rapidly and convincingly with children's literature partly because the post-war period in this country has seen an explosion in the publication of novels written especially for children with the result that some have described this period as the Golden Age of the genre. Writers of the calibre of Rosemary Sutcliffe, Alan Garner, Leon Garfield and William Mayne are writing specifically for children, so there is now a considerable collection of modern children's classics alongside the heritage available for use in our classrooms.

Exploring and using the personal experiences of the pupils

Teachers in secondary schools, unlike those teaching in infant schools, do not always acknowledge that their pupils come to school with a wide variety of experiences and learning, acquired almost as if by a process of osmosis, often haphazardly, in growing up in their homes and neighbourhoods. More often than not these experiences are totally ignored.

In a subject such as the teaching of English, however, where attitudes, values and relationships are, or should be, constantly presented for consideration, personal experiences are of great importance. It is of little use trying to get pupils to make sense of, and to evaluate, let us say, personal relationships in a work of literature, if they are not also invited to test these on the pulses of their own understanding of life. If they are to make considered judgements about people and events, they need help in probing and clarifying their own attitudes and values, and perhaps modifying and deepening them. By doing this they can also be helped to acknowledge and value their uniqueness as individuals, while recognising that they share a commonality of experiences with others. The acknowledgement that pupils have valid experiences outside school, worthy of consideration inside it, also helps to break down the barriers between experiences and knowledge gained in school and those which they are daily building up in their lives at home, and with friends in their neighbourhoods. Moreover, the realisation that too often in school pupils are expected to engage with complex experiences at too abstract a level, has led these teachers to use the personal experiences of their pupils as initial steps to more complex and more generalised explorations of the human condition.

These teachers would also argue that the affective aspects of experience, as well as the cognitive, are important in any school curriculum, although this is not always the case in many schools. By opening up personal values and attitudes for consideration, they argue that it is possible to give the affective its due recognition, and that nowhere is it more appropriate to do this than in the English classroom, where it is possible to merge the affective and the cognitive in a satisfying and harmonious manner. But, of course, it does require the most sensitive, delicate and intelligent teaching. Underlying this approach is the insistence that English must concern itself before all else with the articulation of what is felt most intensely and what is most significant in pupils' lives. It is argued that schools have in general, overtly or covertly, suppressed that kind of voice and, rather than help most pupils in this process, they have convinced them of their linguistic ineptitude, while luring a few towards safe 'essay' work, the vehicle for acceptable ideas, often couched in almost obsolete styles.

The skills or pragmatic approach

The heavy emphasis on reading and writing in schools, partly brought about by traditional attitudes to teaching and learning, partly by the original conception of education in the old elementary schools of minimal literacy and numeracy, and partly by the influence of the examination system and its domination by the universities, has led some teachers of English to concentrate a fair amount of their time on teaching the acquisition of certain limited skills related to reading and writing. Many will probably remember wading through masses of uncontextualised written exercises set by the teacher with the express purpose of increasing the pupil's ability to punctuate and to spell correctly. Hundreds of thousands of incorrect sentences have had to be corrected, nonsense sentences unscrambled, and formal grammar exercises worked through, in the mistaken belief that a descriptive study of language based on Latin will improve written competency, despite the findings of over 70 years research to the contrary. Yet more thousands of isolated comprehension exercises, spelling lists, warnings against spurious Johnsonese, exhortations against the overuse of 'nice' have filled countless exercise books. Endless written exercises have arisen out of the study of literature, hunt the metaphor and spot the simile, mark off the correct feet in lines of poetry, all supposedly testing the pupil's knowledge of the subject. Exercises and questions which have inexorably led to notions of correctness, prescriptions and proscriptions about language, resulting in a dulling of curiosity about how people really use words. Even worse, they have led to an ignoring, even devaluing, of rich and original uses of language, especially those of vernacular speech.

Worthy attempts no doubt to bring about an improvement in literacy, and to prepare the pupil for the world outside of school, but often excrutiatingly dull, and with the additional hazard that many pupils have seen little or no relationship between the acquisition of skills and their other uses of language. It is as if the pupils, once they have arrived in school, were clean slates, upon which the teacher must inscribe the correct rules of writing and reading, or worse, that such language as the pupil possessed was no foundation on which to build, and that an alternative well-behaved and domesticated model needed to be promoted.

But how to fuse a skills approach, which helps all pupils, the backward and the capable, to improve their abilities to use language, with some of the other approaches which we are sketching out, still eludes many teachers of English, even the innovatory. How to teach skills imaginatively and systematically is a long way off in many English classrooms.

A thematic approach

The text-books of the last 20 years provide an excellent guide to the main changes in English teaching. 20 years ago a typical course-book would attempt to provide all the 'language' learning required by a class for a year. In addition to composition topics and endless exhortations, proscriptions and prescriptions, they were crammed with exercises most of which called for one-word or single-sentence answers. Indeed there were well-used text books which consisted of nothing else. They made provision for protracted, often futile industry.

All that has changed, at least in those books which have even the slightest pretension to the accommodation of new ideas. Few text books nowadays would be like this, although one begins to see signs of a return to them since the recent back-to-basics move. Many text books today would be organised on a thematic basis, the themes being of a variety of kinds from animals, heroes, gangs, and the senses, for younger pupils, to parents and children, childhood, work, freedom and authority, and old age, for older pupils. The philosophy, at least in part, underpinning this approach is to bring about the interrelationship of some of the main activities of English in the hope of effecting a greater sense of coherence of the subject in the mind of the pupil. Unlike many approaches in text books of the past, which viewed English as a set of fragmented and compartmentalised exercises — composition on Monday, grammar on Tuesday, comprehension on Wednesday — the thematic approach attempts to relate literature with language, and to show how talking, writing, reading and listening can be used in an interrelated manner, building upon each other into complex explorations of any given theme. Thus a wide variety of activities such as talk of many kinds, drama, writing which ranges from the personal and the imaginative to the factual and the speculative, readings from literature, and research using books of information, can be brought into play in a natural manner, together with a wide variety of different materials, such as extracts from literature, newspapers, recordings from radio, advertisements, official documents, photographs, paintings, illustrations, cartoons and posters. There are few instructions to the pupils in many textbooks of this kind, these being collected together in a Teachers' book with a discussion of the material, and how it might be explored.

By working in this way teachers of English can make room in their classrooms for sustained explorations of serious issues about the human condition which do not rely entirely either upon literary experiences or the personal experiences of the pupil. At the same time, the approach does attempt to cater for a wide variety of pupils, not merely the more able, through the consideration of themes which should quicken the interests of most, and through the multi-variety of approaches and materials which allow for flexibility and variety in teaching.

One clear danger of a too exclusive approach of this kind is that the study of literature can soon become a study of fragmented extracts from literary works, used only to make a point about a theme. If teachers rely too heavily on the readings provided they become vulnerable to the criticism that their pupils never experience, let alone study, a complete novel or play and that the thematic tail wags the literary dog. Literature can be deformed beyond recognition to do thematic service and a poem rich in meanings might be selected for its superficial link with shoes or ships or sealing wax. However, other teachers have chosen to work thematically for the very reason that they can lead their pupils to a wide range of literature because of the interest they have aroused. For a few teachers it has worked in the opposite direction. Suspicious of the resounding abstractions offered in thematic text books (they soon become predictable), they have started with novels or other books and worked outwards from them.

The language approach

The recent interest by some linguists in socio- and psycho-linguistic questions related to education is beginning to have an effect on the way in which some teachers of English view language, and the study of it in their classrooms.

We have shown how the teaching of language has always been a concern of the teacher of English, some of it misguided, some of it brilliantly effective, such as the teaching of literature at its most imaginative. However, some teachers, informed by modern scholarship, have been exploring new ways of teaching and studying language. For them this is now the central concern of the subject. Teachers subscribing to this approach start with the recognition that the pupil arrives at school with competencies in language, and that some of these are considerable. They also recognise that Standard English is one among many varieties, and while accepting its importance do not devalue other forms. They attempt to redress the balance from what they consider to be an undue emphasis on the teaching of literature, by incorporating a wide variety of contextualised explorations of language in their teaching. As they do this they also try to develop the pupil's competencies in spoken as well as written language, in listening as well as reading. These teachers attempt to arouse an interest and fascination in many varieties of language for their own sake, and in the different purposes for which human beings use them. Thus, their teaching concentrates not only on the language which the pupil produces, but also on language used by others as this impinges on him. The focus is less on descriptive grammars of language (though for the older sixteen to eighteen year old pupils this would not be ruled out), but more on how language is used in our everyday lives. The language of the mass media is one obvious area of language usage which is studied: although this has been part of the English curriculum for some time, the emphasis in the early days of study in the 1930s was in the Arnoldian tradition of guarding against its detrimental effects. Other less obvious usages, such as the language of the urban environment, the language of desultory conversation, the language of official reports, the language of children, and so on, would also now be considered worthy of serious study.

Thus an interesting and exciting new study of language is beginning to emerge in English, helped in its impetus by the easy availability of tape recorders, whereby teachers can now bring into their classrooms for contemplation a wide variety of spoken, as well as written language. This work is in its infancy in spite of powerful advocates. Enough has been done, much of it with frankly experimental intent, for others to benefit and for some reformulations to be considered. It is possible, however, to teach new ideas about language as received wisdom, to require pupils to master orders of abstraction for which they are not ready, and to proceed through a presented sequence of units, whether it has all aroused an interest or not. There is no magic charm which guarantees that linguistics-inspired teaching will not be as deadening as any other. It remains a problem to find a way of linking the study of language not only with active learning but also with the productive uses of language. It may be that language study will remain in its own niche with only tenuous links with the rest of English. Yet if the old attractive goal of a unified teaching of English is to be reached, ways will have to be found of making the study of English part of the process of becoming a more proficient user of the mother tongue.

The radical/political approach
The final approach which we discern has only recently begun to emerge, and as yet may still be just on the horizon. Some teachers of English, often working in multi-racial, densely populated, urban, working-class areas of inner cities, have adopted a more radical/political approach to the teaching of their subject. Their political consciousnesses have been aroused, and are constantly fed by what they see to be the exploitation of working people, the unfairness of our society, which is only slowly changing if at all in some respects, the poor housing conditions which many of their pupils live in, the desolation of the local environment, the limited resources, poor facilities and high turnover of staff in their schools, and the unlikely chances of most, if not all of their pupils ever fulfilling their innate abilities and breaking out from the inevitable cycle of deprivation and disadvantage.

This political awareness has led these teachers to encourage their pupils to use their language to question these aspects of their lives, and the socio-political organisations of our society which allow them to continue. The main thrust of their teaching is to make their pupils socially and politically aware, in the hope that they will eventually use this awareness to work within their communities bringing about change. They have been strongly influenced by the de-schoolers' critiques, and the now familiar argument that schools are merely selection mechanisms for feeding roughly the right numbers into the appropriate occupational slots. Only a radical break, they argue, can make any difference. Rejecting the social mobility model of schooling, they want English teaching to emphasise working-class values, traditions and class-consciousness. They see as major resources the families of their pupils, their recollections and activities, and the recent working-class history of their area and its documents.

A less politically aggressive form of this approach is one which encourages the full participation of the local community in the teaching, so that pupils spend some of their time among people such as local craftsmen, traders, housewives, and social workers finding out more about their local environment, and how their community works. Often teaching of English of this kind shades off into social studies and humanities and the subject becomes part of an integrated approach.

Some theories underlying innovatory approaches

Teaching and learning in our schools often takes the form of the teacher telling the pupils something, to be followed by the pupil reproducing in written form what he has been told, so that in due course the teacher can check on whether the pupil has learned what he has told him. It seems clear that this style of teaching, reinforced by the dead hand of an examination system which frequently seems almost perversely to discourage speculative and exploratory thinking, has put a premium on factual knowledge. Some teachers of English are no better or worse than their colleagues in this respect, preferring to deal in certainties and to have quick feedback from their teaching.

The premium on factual knowledge leads teachers, for example, to view writing as a product which displays what is known, and what has been forgotten. Writing as a process, which reveals something of the struggle which the pupil is going through as he tries to learn, is frequently ignored. Yet processes in language are as important as products, and some teachers of English are now coming to realise that there must be a constant interaction between process and product in the pupil's use of language as he struggles to understand new knowledge. For this reason, if for no other, fragments of language, spoken or written, are often as important as polished pieces when real learning is going on.

But these processes are still only dimly understood and precisely how they relate to learning is like looking through a glass darkly. Nevertheless some teachers of English are getting help in understanding them from the insights of socio- and psycho-linguists, as well as from educationists, so in the next section of this paper we propose to sketch out some of the more important theories which inform their teaching. However, we should point out that some of our English classrooms are still caverns of benighted darkness, for some teachers of English are hardly aware of these theories.

Purposes for which we use language

If one were to stop people in the street and ask them why we use language, it is more than likely that most will say to communicate. Pressed to explain in greater detail what this means, the chances are that they will say to communicate thoughts or information to other people. It will probably need a fair amount of probing on our part before they begin to suggest other reasons. This fairly crude notion of language is one which we think many teachers have. It is only in the past decade or so that the multi-variety of different purposes and reasons for our uses of language have begun to be seriously considered in education. The fact that language is used for many different purposes, such as to relate to others, to assert ourselves, to find out information and to explore worlds of the imagination, and that it is determined among other things, by the subject matter under discussion, the context, our relationships to others and our intentions, is only now slowly beginning to be recognised and to influence the teaching of English in our schools.

What has followed from this is that teachers are beginning to consider the curriculum in English not only in terms of content, such as literature, writing, comprehension, and so on, but also in terms of the range of functions of language they ought to foster in their classrooms, and how these might help them to achieve their intentions as teachers of English. It is in this respect that models of language suggested by some linguists have been particularly helpful, for they provide differentiated but reasonably comprehensible and manageable function categories for hard-pressed teachers to use. We have in mind, for example, Halliday's seven functions of language, and Jakobson's hierarchy of functions.

However, the understanding that language serves a variety of functions does not solve the problem of priorities. Clearly all categories are not equal, socially, developmentally and communicatively. Teachers are, therefore, left with the educational decision about how these category systems might best be used to answer these questions, for answers have yet to be found. Perhaps teachers of English and developmental psychologists should try harder to talk to each other.

Dialects, accents and standard English

In a society as class conscious as ours, regional accents and dialects have often been considered debased and aberrant forms of the language. Those who argue like this also argue that in order to use language correctly we must speak in received pronunciation, and write in standard English. Those guardians of 'correct' English still write their letters of complaint to the newspapers about 'bad' English, seeing this as yet further evidence of our decline as a nation. This attitude has its advocates among teachers of English, and it has led to a fair amount of difficulty among both teachers and pupils.

The difficulties have been further compounded by the fact that written standard English is the *lingua franca* of educated people, who when speaking in more formal situations imperceptibly move their language towards standard, and speak more or less in received pronunciation. Standard English is also the *lingua franca* of the international community (although one will find interesting variations on it), it is the form of language found in the majority of publications in this country, the language of text books, and of most teachers when teaching. In short it might be called the language of education, and of the educated. In recent years, however, the work of linguists such as Firth, Labov, Quirk and Trudgill has made teachers more aware of the validity of dialects and regional accents, how they add variety and colour to our language, and how dialect forms are as capable as standard English of conveying complex ideas and feelings.

This realisation has led to an awareness that a person's dialect and accent are an integral part of his personality, and therefore something very personal to him. It is the language form through which his identity and personal relationships are manifested. To attack and debase this is, in some measure, to attack and debase him, his family and his friends. Antipathy to regional speech often conceals another antipathy. As Halliday puts it, 'I don't like his vowels usually means I don't like his values'.

The presence in schools of large numbers of pupils who are speakers of overseas dialects of English has brought into sharp focus an issue which was there all the time. What happens to vernacular speakers in our schools? It is one thing to aim at standard for the written language and quite another to make it (plus received pronunciation) the target for the spoken language. Even for the written language it is no obvious target when the writing is 'literary' (stories, poems, autobiography), as anyone who has read creole stories, for instance, can testify.

Realisations such as these have enabled some teachers of English to be less proscriptive in the classroom, and to be tolerant of dialects and accents, which may be an important first step to building bridges between the language of the home and that of the school, and to a more confident use of standard English.

The pupil's idiosyncratic world view

In the past few years teachers of English have become interested in the relationship between language and thought. The work of linguists such as Sapir and Whorf, the anthropologist Malinowski, and psychologists such as Vygotsky, Luria, Yudovitch, Piaget, Kelly and Bruner have begun to influence the work of some of them. Sapir's contention, for example, that 'human beings do not live in the objective world alone' has been restated in different ways by many interested in teaching and learning. The fact that all of us, even within the same culture and sub-culture, may see aspects of the world differently has been of particular interest. The importance to teachers of English that all of us build up our idosyncratic constructions of events becomes apparent when we remember that part of their concern is the exploration of individual attitudes and values, interpersonal relationships, and many other facets of the human condition, expressed either through literature and other media, or through the re-examination of one's own individual experiences. Explorations of these kinds have not the certainties that explorations in other subjects might yield, and the teacher has to acknowledge that the idiosyncratic experience of each individual will affect the way in which he uniquely probes those experiences which are the concern of the typical English classroom. This has special relevance for all of his work, but nowhere is this more important than in the teaching of literature, where it has to be recognised that response is intimately bound up with the experiences a pupil brings to the text, as well as with the experiences encapsulated within the text itself. Thus, in a sense, there is no one correct response. Granted response has to be within the parameters that the text sets, otherwise the work or the pupil fails (Othello is clearly a jealous man and to say that he wasn't would be ridiculous), but teachers of English are now recognising that within those parameters there is room for a variety of emphases, according to individual response.

What this means, of course, is that received opinions about literature, or about other aspects of the work in English, have to be considered alongside the opinions floating in the classroom. Thus meanings about experiences have to be negotiated rather than imposed. Some anxiety has been expressed that all kinds of irrelevant meanderings are sanctioned by this approach. But many teachers are willing to take that risk preferring it to manifest insincerities or outright rejection. Above all they want pupils to learn to wrestle for meaning, in immature ways if need be rather than attempt to ape (usually in travesty) literary criticism which at its best is a sophisticated and mature activity.

The experience of writing

Recent research into writing has also given teachers of English new insights into some of the processes involved. This research, questioning the time honoured categories of writing derived from classical rhetoric — narrative, exposition, argument and description — has suggested that a different model might be more appropriate. This model, derived from an empirical study of a wide sample of school writing, considers function (what the writing is for), and audience (the view of the teacher the pupil seems to have as he writes). The model suggests three broad function categories, the expressive, the poetic and the transactional with subdivisions of the latter on an abstraction scale, and six broad audience categories, child to self, child to trusted adult, pupil to teacher as partner in dialogue, pupil to teacher as examiner, pupil to other pupils, writer to his readers or public audience.

This research, like any others in the social sciences, has holes in it, but it also has some very suggestive ideas which are helping to inform the teaching of English. Briefly these are firstly, that expressive writing, writing which is like written-down speech and which has many of the characteristics of the kind of language we use when writing or talking to a friend who is interested in us, is an important style whereby pupils make first runs at exploring and coming to terms with new experiences. Secondly, this writing should have its place in secondary schools, rather than be discouraged, as seems to be the case at present. Thirdly, writing which is transactional, that is writing to explain, persuade, advise, theorise and so on, is better understood if considered on an abstraction scale. Fourthly, many transactional written tasks set in school do no more than ask pupils to regurgitate information at a low level of thinking. Fifthly, the sense of audience which the pupil has of his teacher (does he see him as trusted adult or examiner?) will radically affect how he shapes up to the writing task. And finally, the way a teacher sees his role in responding to the written work can affect the kinds of writing tasks he habitually sets. The research had reminded us that teachers too often see their role as setting written tasks which focus on discovering if their pupils have learned something, and then responding as examiners of that learning. They seem to be more interested in receiving neatly finished samples of writing, than being prepared to sanction written work which is the outcome of the process of the struggle to learn and which may well have a less tidy and neatly sewn up look.

Some examples of current practice

The teaching of English has clearly undergone some radical changes in the past two decades, at least among innovatory teachers. Changes in views about the subject will inevitably have brought changes in practice. As a conclusion to this paper we propose to sketch some examples of practices one might find in today's classrooms.

Talking to learn

Teachers have always had a hunch that talking was one way of learning, although frequently their model has been that the teacher did most of the talking and the pupil the listening. However, from time to time the teacher has asked questions, and called for opinions, which suggests that there has been a realisation that pupil talk, however limited, had its value. Some teachers of English now realise that speech is primary and that all of us learn a great deal of what we know through talking things over with others. So in many English classrooms today, teachers are encouraging their pupils to talk among themselves about the work in hand, resulting in small group as well as large class discussions.

Talk of this kind will be concerned with a whole range of aspects of the subject, such as exploring the text of a poem, recalling personal experiences in an anecdotal manner, evaluating a tape recording of a radio interview, creating a radio play, reporting back findings of a small group to the whole class, or answering questions from the teacher. What will be clearly evident is that the talk will be very varied, at times exploratory and hesitant with ideas only partly thought through, sometimes well organised, complex and confident, at times brief and elliptical, sometimes cut and thrust, and at times very collaborative with ideas and opinions being taken up and developed at some length. What will also be clear is that some of the initiative for learning will have been firmly placed in the hands of the pupils, the teachers subscribing to the principle that pupils have to engage with new knowledge in a heuristic manner, at least for some of the time.

Clearly the classroom will look differently from the stereotype of serried ranks of desks facing the blackboard. Pupils will often be in groups, and the atmosphere will be more like that of friends talking matters over, arguing and debating, or sorting out problems. At its best the talk will have taken on some of the characteristics of civilised conversation, where tolerance and mutual respect are highly valued, but where intellectual rigour is expected.

Drama

Centuries of tradition of drama in our schools have ensured that the school play has become an enshrined institution. Most of us will have seen a school performance, far fewer though will have experienced the sweat of rehearsals and the exhilaration of the final production. This has been for the chosen few.

The past 20 years or so, however, has seen an increase in the importance of drama in the teaching of English. The training of drama specialists, the provision of drama studies, the timetabling of periods plus a supporting apparatus of advisers, theatre in education groups, festivals and the like have ensured that drama is now firmly on the map in many schools.

Even school productions are different. Shakespeare and *The School for Scandal* are now not the only plays in the repertoire. Alongside the classical heritage, productions today will include modern, sometimes foreign, even controversial plays, and some schools have become even more experimental, producing what can only be described as projects on contemporary issues, where pupils and teachers have built a large scale production as they have gone along.

Side by side with all this are the intimate and almost unpredictable ways in which drama can just crop up. Drama teachers have shown us how, even within the confines of the classroom, teaching can at any moment move quickly in drama of various kinds, such as improvisation, enacting a text, writing a radio play, or taping a documentary. They have shown us that the dramatic mode, with its combination of speech, movement, gesture and physical juxtaposition is a powerful and natural way whereby pupils can explore the lives and feelings of other people, as well as the art of the dramatist.

Writing as process

The act of writing is a highly abstract activity. It is also a solitary one. Unlike speech where a person is helped to make meanings from the contributions of those he speaks with, a person writing works alone, struggling with his memory and his imagination to discover what he wants to say. And in order to convey his meanings, he will have had to master a complex set of conventions, where spoken words have been substituted by written ones. No wonder many pupils find this difficult, and some almost impossible.

In a complex society such as ours, where writing is at a premium for advancement into skilled work of all kinds, and also into higher education, the teacher of English has a duty to help his pupils to improve their abilities to write for a variety of purposes, whether instrumental or personal. This is clearly no easy task, yet in most schools it is left solely to him to bring this about, teachers of other subjects being unwilling to take on any of the responsibility for this work.

The stark reality of the difficulties that many pupils face as they write has led teachers to experiment with a variety of approaches and methods when preparing pupils for written work. Those who have some understanding of processes are frequently creating opportunities for their pupils to talk over their ideas in small groups, sometimes at length, prior to writing. They are also encouraging them to make notes or jottings which can be referred to when they eventually come to write. At times group writing is encouraged, where pupils help each other to formulate and shape their ideas, thus taking the load off each individual and offering security through the group. When particularly difficult kinds of writing are being attempted, such as arguing a point of view, pupils may be encouraged to make extended notes, which the teacher will discuss, either in groups or individually, prior to giving the go-ahead to write at length. And often the finished pieces will be seen as jumping off grounds for further thinking about the task, for aspects of the writing needing more exact definition can be worked on again after consultation.

Working with literature

We have already made the point that literature is a highly wrought art form. Teachers of English have long realised that many pupils have great difficulty in understanding texts, even those written especially for children. Difficulties arise from a variety of causes, such as archaic vocabulary, the density of the text, dislocations of syntax, the form of the work, differences in sensibilities from one era to another, or the mature vision of the writer. In addition, further problems can arise from the tensions between the culture of many of our pupils and that which seems to be represented through literature, between a popular and folk culture on the one hand, and one which seems to be élitist on the other, although this may be polarising matters too sharply. The fact that many pupils are turned off from reading literature, and the enjoyment which accompanies it, has led some teachers to experiment with different ways of exploring texts. It is no good reading around the class or giving dictated notes to many children. Ways have to be found of engaging their interests in what is, after all, a complex business, if one wants to extend their abilities to read for pleasure and instruction, and to deepen their understanding of how to read with discrimination.

It is for these reasons that teachers of English have been experimenting with more active and enactive ways of exploring texts, alongside literary critical approaches. In classrooms where teachers are prepared to chance their arms, one will find a whole range of activities. Pupils may be turning parts of novels into dramatic readings and perhaps taping them; they may be listening to records of poetry readings or BBC broadcasts about literature; they may be exploring poems through choral interpretations, even setting them to sounds and music; some will be trying to imagine themselves in situations similar to those in a novel perhaps, or rewriting a chapter from a different viewpoint. As they do this, they will, of course, be asking many questions about the meaning of a text, about its form, and the writer's use of language, literary critical questions for sure, but without the drudgery and lifelessness which can so often accompany work in literature.

Conclusion

We must add as a final note that we have found it far from easy to pick our way through the maze of practices in the teaching of English and to attempt to present them coherently, while at the same time doing justice to quite diverse views. We are sure that diversity will continue and that within it there will be confrontations and hostilities. Nevertheless some of the changes we have briefly touched upon are now firmly established and are unlikely to be dislodged. What we are fairly certain of is that it would be possible to construct, from this maze of practices, a curriculum in English which would be dynamic and would meet the needs of secondary pupils. To do this, however, requires a more complex understanding of the subject than many teachers seem at present to possess.

Bibliography

Barnes, D.R. *From communication to curriculum*. Penguin, 1976.

Barnes, D.; Britton, J.; and Rosen, H. *Language: the learner and the school*. 2nd edn. Penguin, 1971.

Britton, J.; Burgess, T.; Martin, N.; Mcleod, A.; Rosen, H. *The development of writing abilities (11–18)*. Macmillan Education, 1975. (Schools Council research studies.)

Burgess, C. and others. *Understanding children writing*. Penguin Education, 1973.

Clements, C.; Dixon, J; and Stratta, L. *Reflections*. Oxford University Press, 1963.

Committee of Inquiry into Reading and the use of English. *A language for life*. HMSO, 1975. (The Bullock Report.)

Creber, J.W.P. *Lost for words: Language and educational failure*. Penguin Education in association with the National Association for the Teaching of English (NATE), 1972.

Dixon, J. *Growth through English set in the perspective of the Seventies*. 3rd edn. Oxford University Press for NATE, 1975. (Oxford Studies in Education 10.)

Doughty, P.S. *Language, 'English' and the curriculum*. Edward Arnold, 1974.

Firth, J.R. *The tongues of men* and *Speech*. Oxford University Press, 1964. (Language and learning 2) reprint of 1937 and 1930 edns respectively.

Goody, J and Stratta, L, eds. 'English in a multi-cultural society.' *English in Education*, 11, 1, 1977.

Halliday, M. 'Relevant models of language.' *Educational Review*, 22, 1, 1969.

Harpin, W.S. *The second R: writing development in the junior school*. Unwin education books 31. Allen & Unwin, 1976.

Holbrook, D. *English for maturity: English in the secondary school*. Cambridge University Press, 1967.

Jakobson, R. 'Linguistics and poetics.' In *Style in language*. Edited by T.A. Sebeok. Technology Press of MIT and John Wiley, 1960, pp 350–377.

Kelly, G.A. *Theory of personality: the psychology of personal constructs*. Norton, 1963.

Labov, W. 'The logic of non-standard English.' In *Language and social context*. Edited by P.P. Giglioli. Penguin, 1972.

Luria, A.R. and Yudovich, F. *Speech and the development of mental processes in the child: and experimental investigation*. Edited by J.S. Simon. Translated from Russian by O. Kovac and J. Simon. Staples Press, 1959.

McGregor, L. and others. *Learning through drama*. Heinemann, 1977.

Malinowski, B. 'Supplement' to *The meaning of meaning*. By C. Ogden and I Richards. Routledge & Kegan Paul, 1923.

Meek, M. and others eds. *The cool web: the pattern of children's reading*. Bodley Head, 1977.

Piaget, J. *The language and thought of the child*. Routledge & Kegan Paul, 1959.

Quirk, R. *The use of English*. 2nd edn. Longman, 1968.

Ridout, R. *English today*. Books 1–4. Ginn, 1947.

Robinson, W.P. *Language and social behaviour*. Penguin Education, 1972.

Rosen, C. and Rosen, H. *The language of primary school children*. Penguin Education for the Schools Council, 1973.

Sapir, E. *Language: an introduction to the study of speech*. Harcourt, Brace, 1921.

Schools Council. *Teaching English to West Indian children*. Evans Methuen Educational, 1970. (Working paper 29.)

Searle, C. *Classrooms of resistance*. Writers & Readers Publishing Cooperative, 1975.

Seely, J. *In context: language and drama in the secondary school*. Oxford University Press, 1976. (Oxford studies in education 12.)

Slade, P. *Child drama*. University of London Press, 1954.

Stratta, L, ed. 'Writing.' *English in education*, vol 3 no 3. NATE in association with Oxford University Press Educational.

Stratta, L; Dixon, J; and Wilkinson, A. *Patterns of language*. Heinemann, 1973.

Thompson, D. 'What is literature?' In 'Eng Lit and English Literature.' *NATE Bulletin*, 3, 2, Summer 1960.

Trudgill, P. *Accent, dialect and the school*. Edward Arnold, 1975.

Vygotsky, L. *Thought and language*. Edited and translated by E. Haufmann and G. Vaker. Massachusetts Institute of Technology Press and John Wiley, 1962.

Way, B. *Development through drama*. Longman, 1967.

Whorf, B. *Language, thought and reality*. Edited by J.B. Carroll. Oxford University Press, 1966.

Wilkinson, A; Stratta, L; and Dudley, P. *The quality of listening: the report of the Schools Council Oracy Project (age range 11–18)*. Macmillan Education, 1974.

3. Languages and minority groups

G.E. Perren

Language and citizenship

In nineteenth century Europe some quite new concepts about race, nationality and nationalism made their appearance. These were closely associated with particular languages and language communities, which thereby assumed a new political importance. The older ideas that religion, dynastic legitimism and strategic geography provided the bases of the State or an adequate political nexus yielded to a new ideal of the nation-state, whose frontiers should coincide with linguistic boundaries, and whose national culture would then be exalted through a national language. Support for this ideal came from most academic philologists: 'Nations and languages against dynasties and treaties, this is what has remodelled, and will remodel still more, the map of Europe' wrote Max Müller in 1862, and he was not alone in such ideas. Linguistic nationalism and a belief in its virtues, even its sanctity, contributed to the liberation of Greece, to the unification of Italy and to the break-up of the Austro-Hungarian Empire. Although often associated with independence, the principle of language could also be used to justify hegemony — Pan-Slavism, Pan-Germanism and Magyarisation. As a factor in 'national self-determination' however, language became unquestioned, and by 1919 was accepted as a guiding principle in re-drawing the map of Europe after the 1914–1918 war. 'It is natural that as a general rule, nationality should be determined by language, for language is an expression, albeit not the only expression, of the national spirit . . .' Such was the view of Thomas Masaryk in 1925[1] with which even the Marxists did not disagree.

Throughout the nineteenth century and after, British governments and British public opinion generally approved of and supported linguistic nationalism in Europe, although not necessarily outside Europe, and being noticeably unenthusiastic about it in Wales, Ireland and Scotland. During the same period, the United States too championed the rights of small nations and of linguistic minorities abroad which wished to become small nations, while within its own borders it was committed to the policy of becoming the great melting pot of European languages and cultures — whose exponent would be English.

The development of language-linked nationalism and language-determined nationality in Europe coincided with the expansion of state education and adult literacy. The two processes were not unconnected; as new schools were set up, new questions arose about which languages should be used in them. Although the wider spread of education was not always associated with the progress of liberalism or democracy (as commonly believed in Britain), it often coincided with and accelerated a shift of power away from traditional ruling classes.

The last 150 years in Europe have amply demonstrated that there is no necessary connection between linguistic autonomy and political liberty. The unification of Germany on linguistic lines aided Hohenzollern imperialism no less than Nazi racism.

45

In some countries the linguistic chauvinism of majorities led to the suppression of minorities — often in the guise of self-determination for some at the expense of others. It became clear that people can equally be oppressed in any language — including their own. They can also achieve political or social freedom in any language — not necessarily their own. They can do so through membership of societies which require them to learn a new language — as millions have done in the United States. It is as true today as in the past that if language autonomy can begin as a liberal principle, it can easily be transformed into an authoritarian doctrine. This process in Europe has been summarised:

> Nationalism involved a belief in the identification of the nation, as a community with a traditional culture of its own, and the state. Where the identity was not perfect, it had to be made so. Hence the attempts by ruling nations to assimilate by force any minorities unhappy enough to find themselves in their power. In movements such as Germanisation, Russification, Magyarisation and so on, European nationalism developed into a kind of petty imperialism. (Cobban, 1970)

Britain, of course, has never been a nation-state in the modern European sense; its unifying principle has remained primarily geographical and dynastic. There has been, and still is, English nationalism, Welsh nationalism and Scottish nationalism — not to mention Irish nationalism. Each of these has invoked language among its past and present tribal gods to varying degrees. But there has never been a characteristic *British* nationalism, while overseas British imperialism was only incidentally language-linked. It is true that around 1900 there was a short-lived ideological notion of an 'Anglo-Saxon' race and language, embracing both Britain and the United States. Vestiges of this are still discernible in odd romantic movements of no great political significance, and its ghost is sometimes raised as a kind of chimera to serve as a target for other more corporeal nationalisms.

The spread of English as a world language has not been motivated by any consistent political or cultural ideology. If English was used as the language of imperialism in India, it also became the language of anti-imperialism, there and elsewhere. In most colonial territories, there was no consistent educational policy about the use of English. British colonial administrations were far more often accused of 'keeping English from the natives' than of forcing it on unwilling learners. In Africa, indeed, they tried hard but unsuccessfully to 'develop' the vernacular languages. In contrast, French colonial administrations consistently maintained the unique civilising mission of the French language and its culture, insisting on its use in schools and paying little attention to indigenous tongues.

Languages of wider communication such as English, French, Spanish, Swahili and Arabic have, outside Europe, helped to build new states out of multilingual communities, providing the means of political, economic and social cohesion as well as of educational development. The use of such languages has helped to avoid dangers of language 'Balkanisation', particularly in the newer states of Africa. But the linguistic backwash of European nationalism or of anti-colonialism has also led to such odd proposals as making Swahili the national language of all Africa (Taiwo, 1976). A

46

common mother-tongue has, of course, never been a sure indicator of a common nationality, although a common second language may be an essential aid to common citizenship. The pragmatic examples of Belgium and Switzerland are as instructive as the doctrinal complexities of the Soviet Union and the overt simplicity of the United States in matters of language policy.

In spite of idealised assumptions by some that they are based on single languages, nearly all states are and always have been multilingual in the sense that they have included linguistic minorities within their borders. Most, whether federal or centralised, have made educational and legal provision for such minorities. In some the 'equal' rights of minority languages are 'guaranteed' to such an extent by constitutional law as to cast doubt on its effectiveness (Desheriyev and Mikhalchenko, 1976). 'Equality' among languages in a multilingual community seems a rather nebulous concept since no-one can ensure that all languages are equally used, equally useful or equally productive. Sheer necessity sometimes dictates pragmatism, as in India where although fourteen Indian languages have been given 'equal' constitutional status, English retains *de facto* a place no longer appropriate *de jure* simply because it is of essential practical value. In many countries decisions about the language(s) to be used in schools are taken regionally, provincially or locally, even when for purposes of administration or higher education one or more national or official languages have been established.

New social and political pressure may revive demands for the use of a language whose legal status has become dormant or overlaid by demographic changes, as in Canada. A new interpretation of existing constitutional law may have sudden implications for languages in education, as in California. International organisations adopt languages for their own administrations and operations according to varying notions of power politics, community of interest or the needs of public relations: the United Nations uses five, the Council of Europe two or three, the European Community seven at present.

Whatever the historical causes — and they are many and conflicting — recently there has been an upsurge of interest in the preservation and extension of the use of children's mother tongues in their education, at the same time as the practical need to learn second languages has increased throughout the world. These two phenomena are complementary rather than conflicting. Bilingualism, in an infinity of forms, but all involving the active *use* of two languages, is becoming the norm for many millions. Up to half the world's population may be bilingual to some degree; but of these the majority acquire their bilingualism *outside* school without benefit of formal teaching. On questions of linguistic pluralism in education most governments at least profess principles and many have policies. Britain recognises the bilingual principle in Wales and in the remoter parts of Scotland, but schools in England are obstinately and officially deemed monoglot.

In England attitudes towards the languages of resident minorities are coloured by social, historical and local prejudices and experiences. This gives an impression of varying prestige being accorded to different languages: some seem more respectable than others in popular esteem. No doubt much depends on the socio-economic status of their speakers. German, Spanish, Polish and Italian may be rated above Greek,

Turkish and Chinese, and these above Punjabi, Gujarati, Bengali and Urdu. How far the commonwealth origin of languages, or the colour of their speakers, affects attitudes is a matter for speculation.

Widespread lack of sensitivity or sympathy towards the languages of recent immigrants may exist because Britain has not yet fully adjusted to the paradox of remaining a long-term exporter of English to the rest of the world while becoming a major importer of non-English speaking citizens. For, if the outside world so obviously wants to learn English, why should those who choose to come and live here permanently wish to retain any other language? Clearly, however, some do. This cannot be regarded merely as the affair of the individuals concerned since it affects many children at school and the educational provision to be made for them. We must clarify principles and determine a policy in Britain, just as other multilingual states have had to do. The need has become more pressing because of the European Community's directive that its member states must provide for the mother-tongue education of migrant workers. In Britain any such provision made for migrant workers must affect all linguistic minorities. Educational discrimination between the children of migrant, immigrant and resident citizens is as undesirable as impractical.

Although in Britain language has no specific relationship to citizenship in any legal sense, it remains a prominent factor in our imprecise perception of differences of race and nationality. As a footnote to this section, we might ponder the statement made over a hundred years ago by an eminent British historian:

> If we take the establishment of liberty for the realisation of duties to be the end of civil society we must conclude that those states are substantially the most perfect which . . . include various distinct nationalities without oppressing them . . . A state which is incompetent to satisfy different races condemns itself: a state which labours to neutralise, to absorb or to˙expel them destroys its own vitality: a state which does not include them is destitute of the chief basis of self-government. (Lord Acton, 1862)

The newer mother-tongues of Britain

At present there are no reliable figures of the total numbers who speak particular languages and of their distribution in Britain. More important for educational planning, there are none to indicate their age range. The last census, of 1971, showed the total number of *overseas-born* to be over three million — or around six per cent of the total population. To these must be added new arrivals since 1971 and children born in Britain who continue to speak their parents' language. Of the overseas-born a considerable proportion speak English as their mother tongue, although this may be a dialect, like that of many West Indians.

Census returns show the birthplace of individuals, but this is not a reliable guide to language. Immigrants from East Africa are more likely to speak Gujarati or Punjabi than an African language, although they may also speak some Swahili as a second language as well as some English. Immigrants from Cyprus may speak either Turkish or Greek, those from Hong Kong Hakka or Cantonese, those from the Indian sub-continent a wide range of different languages. Most countries of Asia and Africa are plurilingual. In Europe, country of origin provides a better although not infallible guide to language, and it is reasonable to assume that the German-born speak German, the Spanish-born Spanish and the Italian-born some variety of Italian. The most numerous mother tongues of the foreign-born and their descendants in Britain are Punjabi, Urdu, Bengali, Gujarati, German, Polish, Italian, Greek, Spanish and Cantonese. But within some of these groups there may be extensive dialect variations, and among illiterates this may complicate any attempt at categorisation by language. Linguistic minorities tend to concentrate in large towns, most notably in London, although the Chinese are much more widely scattered than, for example, Urdu or Punjabi-speakers.[2]

Not all minority groups are of recent arrival. There are long-established communities of Poles, Hungarians, Latvians and Ukrainians which have carefully maintained their cultural identity and languages. Many came originally as political exiles, which probably strengthens their attachment to their own languages. Rather different is the origin of Jewish groups, emigrating originally from many areas of Eastern Europe, but linking themselves into a community here by a common use of Yiddish. And, of course, in the nineteenth century a remarkable assortment of political refugees sought asylum in Britain; although these hardly constituted linguistic minorities in themselves, they often induced considerable respect for their languages among the British who sympathised with their political views. Much earlier, in the seventeenth century, there had been sizeable immigrations of French and Flemings who established settled communities with their own religious and cultural institutions. However, as an educational problem for maintained schools, the presence in Britain of large numbers of non-English speaking or bilingual children is essentially a recent development, largely associated with the inflow from Commonwealth countries of those possessing common citizenship of the United Kingdom and with it the right to a permanent domicile here.

Attitudes to English

Attitudes of minorities towards adopting English as their language of education and employment — although not as necessarily that of their family or social life — may reflect the linguistic and educational history of their country or origin. For Indians, Pakistanis and Africans, English already had a high status in their homelands. Many of them came from traditionally multilingual societies where education above the most elementary level was not available in their own mother tongue and had in any case to be acquired through a second language. Those from India may have had experience of the 'three language formula' in their own education. In Commonwealth countries the use of English for official and commercial purposes, as a medium of secondary and higher education and as the general means of occupational advancement, was normal. However, in these same countries the use of English in education is now becoming *relatively* less widespread as schools become more numerous and less selective. So demands from some minority groups of Asian or African origin for greater recognition of their own mother tongues in their education in Britain may reflect the increasing use of the same languages in schools in their homelands, or mirror the development of 'national' languages in some of them. On the other hand, they may be asking for a recognition in Britain of language 'rights' believed to have been denied them at 'home' — sometimes this is less a reaction to personal experience than to a deprivation ascribed to their communities by political hindsight.

The attitude of those originating from predominantly monolingual European countries is of course different. In Italy and Spain, for example, English has no very long standing as a curriculum subject in schools, and has certainly not in the past been regarded as a better means for educational, social or even cultural advancement than Italian or Spanish. Only recently has English acquired an obvious commercial, scientific and technical value to many occupational groups in Europe and become the most widely learned foreign language among all classes. For the young it has an internationalised cultural attraction, but one often unrelated to traditional literary or educational values.

In Britain the attitude of central and local education authorities towards the language needs of minority groups has been quite simple: the original prescription was a good dose of English as a foreign language, to be administered when and where convenient. Thus there has been developed by the Schools Council one collection of course material, *Scope*, with various stages, to provide for the generality of non-English speakers. To many administrators it was hard to believe that with all our experience of teaching the rest of the world English, we could not easily teach it to the minorities in our midst. But there was an inbuilt paradox: the overseas learners of English had often been highly selected, highly motivated and taught by single-minded trained specialists. In Britain often none of these advantages applied.

Estimating needs

A national inventory of the total numbers and distribution of all children in Britain with mother tongues other than English would be of great value, the more so if their individual languages could be identified and classified. Classification of languages for educational purpose presents special difficulties. Almost unlimited distinctions can be made linguistically between 'different' languages and dialects of languages, especially those of India. But working definitions of what may constitute viable languages for *educational* purposes are needed — those suitable for pedagogical use — and in these definitions linguistic, cultural, religious and social criteria must be applied. There would be formidable difficulities in constructing a complete national picture and in keeping it up to date. It is not yet clear how stable — in a geographical sense — the location of newer minority groups will prove, although with the exception of Chinese-speakers it seems that major groups, once established in particular towns, may remain there without dispersing for some time. For practical purposes, localised information might be more useful, since local authorities have to plan and organise education. Doubtless many local authorities already have access to information about the size and nature of minorities, although this may not have been assembled or used for educational purposes and provides little indication of language needs. There is poor coordination of such information and a lack of awareness of the true dimensions of linguistic diversity. Estimates of the total numbers with 'inadequate English' are much more common than estimates of the numbers within separate minority groups.

This rather negative attitude is very revealing: educational authorities are more concerned with establishing how many children do *not* speak English than with how many *do* speak any particular mother tongue. But they should also make it their business to know how many already speak Punjabi, Italian or any other mother tongue *and* are learning or need to learn English. The fact of bilingualism must be recognised: teaching children English as a second language does not thereby erase their mother tongue; it makes them bilingual. Development of bilingualism is thus already undertaken in many English schools, often blindly and nearly always inefficiently. The question is how best to improve it.

The present role of mother tongues in schools

At present there is no general provision for the use, maintenance or recognition of non-English mother tongues in maintained schools. There is insufficient information to decide how far this results from deliberate policy, from administrative constraints, from innate conservatism or from ignorance of linguistic facts.

The views of teachers vary. Some do not encounter the problem; some wish it did not exist. Of those in schools with large numbers of minority children, many say they would like to see more attention paid to children's mother tongues. On exactly how this should be done, there is no great agreement. Few teachers would support the use of languages other than English as general media of instruction; some would like to see them established as curriculum subjects; others press rather vaguely for more 'recognition' of the pupils' own languages, but accept no commitment to teach or use them — or even to identify them.

The views of minority-group parents are no doubt highly variable, but many feel that the first priority must be effective education in English, which must not be prejudiced. Some would need to be convinced that mother-tongue studies would actually aid their children's education or assist their performance in English, as many teachers maintain.

A question sometimes asked is whether minorities will in time abandon their own language and become linguistically integrated to the extent of becoming monolingual in English. This seems more likely to happen among individuals dispersed among English-speakers than among those living within established ethnic communities. In any case there is evidence that language revivalism — a desire to re-learn a 'lost' mother tongue or dialect — can occur.

It would be rash to generalise about the views of organised communities, since they have not been systematically sought, may not have been consciously developed and cannot be dissociated from political, social and religious factors. While parental opinion about the curriculum usually concentrates on practical need and material advantages for their own children, communal views are likely to be less pragmatic and more doctrinaire. It is not unusual for people to hold one view about what is good for others' children and quite a different one about what is good for their own.

Attitudes of native English-speaking parents towards the encouragement or use of 'immigrant' languages in school could be highly charged by local community tensions. This may be a matter on which it is extremely difficult to distinguish between cause and effect. If a particular languge is not taught in schools, it may thereby remain *déclassé*; if it is taught, it may arouse a kind of monolingual backlash. The question of language status arises. Suggestions that English-speaking pupils should be encouraged to learn minority group languages as foreign language options in schools gain little support; in any case their appeal is uneven — it can be assumed that Italian would have more attraction than Punjabi and Spanish more than Gujarati. Quite apart from the relative difficulty of the languages, it seems possible that when a language is labelled 'ethnic' — ie spoken by a large resident minority — it has a lower status than one already labelled 'foreign' ie observably spoken abroad.

The administrative difficulties of providing for non-English mother tongues in the curriculum are daunting to LEAs. Schools with the highest proportion of minority children often have the greatest variety of languages among them. Those containing pupils with fifteen or sixteen different mother tongues have been reported. It is not surprising that sometimes no attempt is made even to identify all the different languages spoken. This may be deliberate — on grounds of non-discrimination, whatever that may mean. Some authorities, like some heads of schools, probably just do not wish to know how complex their linguistic mixture may be and remain content to recognise only a single category of non-English speakers. Experimental work on a small scale by some local authorities should not be overlooked, although no great success for them can yet be claimed, and they certainly do not indicate sudden enlightenment on the part of education committees or the generality of ratepayers.

It is occasionally argued that if equal provision cannot be made for all non-English mother tongues, then it should be made for none, on the grounds that selected groups should not be unduly favoured. Such egalitarianism becomes discriminatory if we accept that the task of schools is to make the best arrangements they can for as many pupils as possible according to their needs. It may well be that compromises about certain languages would be necessary for practical reasons. For some children the only option might be to learn a language similar to but not precisely the same as their own, or the 'national' language of their homeland, rather than a particular and perhaps obscure communal language or dialect. While it seems unlikely that Britain could, like Sweden, make it obligatory for LEAs to offer all children tuition in their own mother tongue, so few statements of principle or intent have been made in Britain that it is hard to avoid the impression that the matter is publicly avoided. The Bullock Report, for example, while quite outspoken about the desirability of 'nurturing' children's bilingualism was noticeably reticent about how this should be done. The Schools Council has expressed no clear views on this issue and its subject committee structure provides no place for the discussion of any mother tongue other than English or Welsh. Research studies on children's communicative skills in Britain has been confined to English-speakers. Home/school contrast studies are more often expressed in terms of rather superficial cultural differences than in those of funda-mental linguistic divergence. *Multicultural* has become popular jargon — providing a taxonomic escape from the reality of multilingualism. Discussions of 'language' in education refer only to English. 'Immigrant languages' have a quite different status from 'modern languages', and are of little concern either to teachers of English or to teachers of foreign languages in Britain.

Extra-curricula provision

That extensive provision is made for language teaching or language maintenance by minority groups outside the maintained school system has been very clearly indicated[3], although no comprehensive or nation-wide picture is yet available. The demand is considerable, as the numbers of children attending evening and week-end classes amply show, but the content, methodology and effectiveness of the teaching thus provided is highly variable. Material support given to such activities ranges from direct financial aid from abroad (eg by the Spanish and Italian governments) to self-help by local communities through subscriptions, with or without minor assistance from LEAs — such as making premises available. The reasons why children attend mother-tongue classes, and the attitudes of parents and communities towards them require detailed study.

What may be called the educational interaction between full-time education in maintained schools and part-time additional classes of this kind requires urgent investigation. Many teachers in maintained schools are unaware of the existence of mother-tongue classes attended by their pupils, let alone of what is taught in them. Some LEAs have no clear picture of what is being provided in their own areas.

The question is complex. Extra-curricula classes may fulfil a very useful task which maintained schools cannot or do not wish to assume. But some control over their activities seems desirable on educational grounds if only to ensure that what is being done in one supports rather than conflicts with what is being done in the other. This may be particularly important for younger children. Direct intervention may not be possible — or desirable — for legal and administrative reasons, unless some form of financial aid were to be given which would warrant laying down qualifying standards for its award. Another possible method of providing beneficial control over the content of what is taught would be to establish recognised examinations (eg at CSE level) suitable for those studying their languages *as mother-tongues*, for which children could be prepared both inside and outside the maintained system, or if necessary individually at home. This would be valuable, too, in enhancing the status of various languages and help to remove some prejudices against their recognition. There seems no reason why guidance should not be given at levels lower than CSE, particularly on the development of reading skills, for example. And among the current concern about improving the teaching of reading in English, one misses any reference whatsoever to the special (and widespread) needs of minority children who may at the same time be learning to read in both English and their mother tongue.

Social attitudes

The social role of minority group languages in Britain seems to have been little studied by linguists or educationists. The assumption by educationists that good English is the prime need to ensure good employment prospects is supported by the views of employers and by provision for teaching English within industry. Vocationally, ineffective English can be a handicap and it is right that schools should recognise this. But it is possible that in some occupations bilingualism can be an advantage (eg in the catering trades) when these employ or provide for particular groups.

The comparative monolingualism of many Asian women in Britain is often referred to, although it is sometimes claimed that this is likely to pass within a generation. In the meantime it exists and certainly colours the attitude of many native-English speakers towards some minorities. Native-English attitudes to 'ethnic' languages range from ignorance and indifference through tolerance to positive resentment. There is little evidence of efforts by public servants or teachers to learn them. Whether more explicit social recognition of multilingualism would be socially divisive or unifying seems to remain a matter of uninstructed opinion rather than a subject for serious investigation. It is likely, however, that a better recognition of individual bilingualism would be distinctly cohesive, and enhance benefits now somewhat speciously attributed to cultural diversity. For at present much lip-service is paid to the assumed virtues of multi-culturalism; in schools a patronising interest in exotic food or clothes is certainly common enough; however, informed interest in the languages which go with them is much more unusual.

Apart from the educational advantages to the individual of recognising and using his bilingualism more effectively, the value to society of maintaining all languages must not be overlooked. The advantage of having among its citizens educated speakers of other languages than English, as a national resource, is being increasingly recognised in the United States and elsewhere. It would be short-sighted to neglect its potential in Britain, if only as a commercial asset, while it is faintly ludicrous to observe would-be linguists travelling thousands of miles to learn or study languages which are spoken on their door-steps by fellow-citizens.

Educational proposals

Two organisations have issued statements on the practical educational issues involved in establishing a place for non-English mother tongues in the general curriculum. A policy paper produced by the National Association for Multiracial Education (NAME) is reproduced below as Appendix 1. Apart from a reasoned statement of educational values, it contains specific proposals for research.

Recently there has been established a voluntary Co-ordinating Committee for Mother Tongue Teaching (CCMTT), which includes representatives of minority groups. It aims to encourage and support the introduction of mother tongues in maintained schools and elsewhere. Its aims and proposals are reproduced below as Appendix 2. They stress particularly the need for more detailed information.

Notes

1 Masaryk, T. G. *The making of a state* 1929, p. 30.
The idea of 'one state one language' has survived two world wars: cf Charles A. Ferguson *Background to second language problems* 1962:

> It is tacitly assumed by many that one of the features of ideal nationhood is the possession of a standardised national language. The absolute ideal would apparently be a language which has a community of native speakers coterminous with the national boundaries and which has a single accepted norm

of pronunciation, spelling, grammar, and vocabulary, used for all levels of speaking and writing, including both a unique national literature and work in modern science.

2 Campbell-Platt, Kiran 'Distribution of linguistic minorities in Britain' in *Bilingualism and British education* CILT, 1976. (CILT Reports and Papers 14) A valuable article, which exposes the difficulties of collecting and analysing existing information on the subject as well as summarising the available data.

3 Khan, Verity S. 'Provision by minorities for language maintenance' in *Bilingualism and British education* CILT, 1976. The first and at present the only published survey of the various schemes operated by minorities themselves. Three urban areas were examined in detail but some idea of the national picture can be obtained from this pioneer study originally supported by the Runnymede Trust. (+ tenth)

References

Lord Acton, *Nationality* 1862.

Cobban, A. *France since the revolution*. 1970, p. 166.

Desheriyev, Y. and Mikhalchenko, V.Y. 'The Soviet experience with languages.' In *Prospects*, VI, 3, 1976:

> 'Equality of all languages is the corner stone of the Soviet Union's language policy.' Every citizen has complete freedom 'to speak and to bring up and educate his children in any language, ruling out all privileges, restrictions or compulsions in the use of this or that language.'

Müller, M. *The science of language*. 1862. p. 12.

Taiwo, T.W. 'Nigeria: language problems and solutions.' In *Prospects*, VI, 3, 1976. The proposal is ascribed to the Nigerian author and playwright Wole Soyinka.

Appendix 1

Submission by the National Association for Multiracial Education to the National Congress on Languages in Education

The general aim of the National Association for Multi-Racial Education is:

> . . . to play an active role in making the changes required in the education system which will further the development of a just multi-racial society.

The Association contends that, in order to effect changes, there needs to be:

> . . . a stronger emphasis on the crucial role that language plays in learning.

As there is now a great deal of evidence that language does play a significant role in the learning process for indigenous children it is important to recognise that the same applies to mother tongues of non-indigenous children.

This Association believes that children who can use their mother tongue and English equally effectively are in a position to make a unique contribution to our society, and therefore encouragement and resources should be provided to support development of the mother tongue.

We believe that there are also definite educational, psychological and social benefits to be gained from the learning of and the use of non-indigenous mother tongues within the educational system. There are two aspects:

(a) the learning of and maintenance of mother-tongues;

(b) use of mother tongue as a medium of instruction.

Priority should be afforded to (a) as mother-tongue deprivation would invalidate its use as a medium of instruction.

Educational

(i) Use of mother tongue in the early pre-school years could accelerate conceptual development as the children would not be expected to handle new learning experiences in terms of a second language.

(ii) Learning processes would be eased if children were not in a situation where they had to listen to instructions in a second language, translate into first and then respond in the second language.

(iii) Direct communication between teacher and child who possess a common mother tongue would be of particular benefit to the slower child.

(iv) The mother tongue is likely to remain the child's best means for organising and expressing his deepest emotions and imagination, and should be respected and developed for this purpose.

(v) Maintenance and development of mother-tongue could develop confidence in a child's ability to learn a second or third language.

Psychological

The use of a child's own mother tongue in school would:

(i) heighten morale;

(ii) increase confidence in ability to learn;

(iii) improve self-concept;

(iv) affect attitude towards all curriculum subject;

(v) raise the development of reasoning/intellectual skills.

Social

(i) The use of mother tongues in school in terms of learning, maintenance or as a medium of instruction would help all teachers and children to respect the values of cultures other than their own.

(ii) There would be an increased awareness that languages other than English have crucial roles.

(iii) Mother-tongue maintenance would ensure the perpetuation of cultural identity and enhance family unity.

(iv) Non-indigenous children should be given the option of learning their mother tongues to the stage of literacy as they are more likely to visit their home countries than (say) France or Germany; they would gain an additional qualification which might help redress the balance of disadvantage, and they would be in a better position to perform useful bilingual roles in a multi-cultural society.

Recommendations

This Association believes that extensive research into the teaching and use of mother tongues within the education system is urgently required. Such action-research would be in the spirit of the EEC draft directive/recommendation under discussion by the Council of Ministers, and could, very possibly, be supported from the funds of the EEC Social Programme. Cooperation with comparable action research programmes in the EEC and other countries would be valuable.

Areas for investigation include:

(i) the relationship between the acquisition of the mother tongue and a second language at all stages of development;

(ii) the relationship between language and conceptual development in bilingual children;

(iii) the optimum methods for maintaining the mother tongue and developing the second language at all stages of development. This Association recognises that a variety of approaches are possible, for example:

(a) the use of mother tongue as a medium of instruction for pre-school or nursery school children;

(b) the maintenance of mother tongue within the primary schools with bilingual teaching techniques in operation;

(c) the provision of examination courses in secondary schools as foreign language options in order to cater for the non-native languages represented in the school;

(d) the use of mother tongue in vocational training courses at colleges of further education or colleges of higher education;

(e) the use of mother tongue as a means of achieving a more rapid adjustment to a new environment and way of life for adolescents newly arrived from overseas.

(iv) The relationship between learning to read and write in the mother tongue and the second language, and the optimum methods for introducing literacy in either language to bilingual children.

(v) The relative merits and disadvantages at all stages of development of teaching the first or second language as a separate item in the school curriculum and of using either as a medium of instruction 'across the curriculum'.

(vi) The logistical problems in catering for relatively scattered minorities (eg the Chinese in Britain), and for the varieties of different languages, dialects and scripts among the minorities whose settlement is more concentrated (eg the wide variety of spoken and written language used by immigrants from the general area of the Punjab in India and Pakistan).

(vii) The relationship between the responsibilities of the maintained school system and the voluntary educative efforts of minority communities, in mother-tongue teaching and other aspects of cultural 'maintenance'.

(viii) The initial and in-service training of teachers to serve in an education service with positive commitment to multi-racial education and clear policies for multi-lingual education.

Appendix 2

Co-ordinating Committee for Mother-Tongue Teaching

1 Consists of a steering group and six sub-committees.

2 Its aims are:
   (a) to introduce mother-tongue provision in the mainstream school;
   (b) in the short term and where this is not possible for numerical and geographical reasons, to support existing provision and encourage new viable schemes.

3 The Co-ordinating Committee will pursue these aims with a secular and non-political approach. We are concerned with all children who are living in, and growing up in, two linguistic environments; their educational, emotional, psychological and social needs. We acknowledge the crucial importance of skill in English but we do not accept that this is incompatible with a maintained and developed skill in the mother tongue. There is evidence that competence in the mother tongue need not interfere with and can positively enhance acquisition of English.

4 The Co-ordinating Committee supports mother-tongue provision for the following reasons:

Every *child* should have the right to full development of his/her existing skills and educational potential. The mother tongue is an essential component of his/her identity and culture. At present children of linguistic minorities are forfeiting several years of their conceptual and linguistic development due to lack of recognition and provision in mainstream school. This provision would help children to maintain a consistent picture of themselves and their family and would decrease the gulf between home and school.

Recognition of the mother tongue would help *teachers* to develop a trusting and confidential relationship with their minority pupils. When minority children and their parents are no longer made to feel ashamed of their mother tongue or inadequacy in English, parent-teacher contact is likely to improve. These factors will help to bridge the gaps between home and school, and mother-tongue school and mainstream school.

Without mother-tongue provision *the school* cannot claim to be a truly comprehensive or neighbourhood school, nor is it recognising this logical extension of the notion of multi-cultural education.

Mother-tongue maintenance and development can avoid an added tension experienced by many minority *families*. That is, it facilitates communication between parents and children, and children and other relatives both in Britain and in the homeland. It is also an important means of understanding the home culture and religion.

For our *society* in general mother-tongue recognition and development is a step toward being a multi-cultural society, and one in which minority languages and cultures have higher status. The option of learning the mother tongue would allow the minorities to develop their own identity as they choose. Instead of encouraging and developing minority languages our society makes these languages into a handicap. The diversity on minority languages in our country is a national resource.

5 To achieve our aims we propose to take the following steps:
   (a) to promote awareness and discussion of the complexities of the issues nationally and at all levels (policy makers, educationists and communities);
   (b) to help collect information and monitor existing provision (voluntary and statutory);
   (c) to encourage contact between existing voluntary organisations, individuals and other organisations interested in promoting this issue;
   (d) to support existing initiatives and to co-ordinate efforts of individuals and organisations.
6 The six sub-committees are: (1) Statutory provision; (2) Voluntary provision; (3) Contact with parents/community organisations; (4) Materials and teacher training; (5) Collecting of information; (6) Monitoring.

4. Language as a curriculum study

E.W. Hawkins

The study of language omitted from the school curriculum

Man is, Jean Aitchison has reminded us (1976), the only 'articulate mammal'. His language is the uniquely human characteristic on which cultural evolution has depended. One would expect the school curriculum to reflect this, but does it?

In addition to study of the universe (the natural sciences, mathematics) most aspects of human *behaviour in groups* have come to have an accepted place in the curriculum. The history of the formation of our human groupings; their interaction with the geography and the ecology of the habitat; the statements that our society has evolved about ethics (not, alas, its best practice which is a harder lesson to teach); the literature, music, dance and drama of our society, and occasionally those of our neighbours; the handicrafts, architecture, domestic science of our community; all these have taken their place in the curriculum. Increasingly in recent years economics and politics have been added (as well they might for, in a democracy whose existence hangs on an intricate industrial and financial machinery, the degree of ignorance and prejudice which motivates the voters who make the ultimate choices is hair-raising).

These aspects of the life of our social group do not have to make their claim to be studied in the curriculum. Their place is accepted and the only discussion is about the best methods and materials to use, how to assess the learning and how to train the teachers. Yet the essential aspect of group behaviour on which the rest depends, namely language, is not a curriculum subject. Language as an aspect of human behaviour is not methodically studied though some aspects may be incidentally, and haphazardly, broached in the course of acquiring and using the mother tongue or, more probably in the foreign language lesson.

Most teachers of English and many teachers of foreign languages are not equipped by their training to discuss language as an aspect of human behaviour. Of course the curriculum does give a large place to 'English' but does this provide the education in *language* that is needed? This is the central question for the present discussion. We need to look at the evidence of neglect of language study in the community. We should then look at one remedy recently advocated and ask if reform of the teaching of English is enough, or whether we need a new component in the curriculum.

Some effects of the omission of language from the curriculum

Parents

There is a crippling lack of awareness among many young parents of the process of language acquisition by their babies. Contrast the excellent school courses in hygiene, diet, domestic economy, biology with most parents' insensitiveness and lack of sophistication in listening to their infants' language. How many parents appreciate

61

the role that dialogue with parents, grandparents and other adults can play in the child's early conceptual/linguistic experience? Gina Armstrong's project in a Yorkshire mining village (see G. Smith, *editor*, 1975) showed what a revelation it could be to young mothers (and fathers) when she led them, by example, to pay closer attention to what two year-olds were trying to communicate. Margaret Donaldson's researches and the many other studies that she draws on in *Children's minds* (1978) indicate what a disadvantage it is for the pre-school child to have a background in which 'awareness of language' is not encouraged. *Language acquisition*, studied through listening to pre-school children and to tapes and videotapes, could be an important element in a secondary school language study course for teenagers who will be parents within a very few years.

Mindless verbiage

Further evidence of the neglect of language study in the curriculum can be seen in widespread tolerance of slipshod use of language. This in its turn seems to reflect a general lack of sophistication regarding language shown, for example, in the wording of official forms, in the acceptance of pointless circumlocutions, or of unnecessary pseudo-technical jargon. The plea we are making is that it should be a central aim of the curriculum to equip pupils to enjoy more fully, and to understand at least partially, what being an articulate mammal could really mean.

The search for short cuts

Naïveté about how language works provides fertile ground in which nostrums and 'short cuts' can find support—eg the generous and well-meant pleas of the Esperanto lobby. One project in a secondary school language study might well be to go back to Saussure's wise comments on Esperanto: 'Artificial languages cease to be controlled by their creators the moment they are put into circulation. From that moment the creator is powerless to preserve their original form, the meanings attached to their words, etc. Esperanto is an attempt of this kind. If it succeeds (in being widely circulated) can it escape the inevitable rule?' (1915). Another project in the same vein might be to discuss the limitations of translation from one language to another, preferably taking examples contributed by pupils in the school who speak minority languages.

Ignorance of the history of native and immigrant languages

There is a general ignorance of the history of English and of the other languages spoken in the British Isles and of the developments that have given them their present form. The place names that surround us and that could enrich travel and exploration in our homeland mean very little to our school leavers, or to their teachers, for lack of study of the history of the languages spoken in the British Isles. What is known about Welsh or Gaelic by the average English adult? How many schools are able to exploit the opportunity offered by the presence of minorities from eg India, Europe, the Mediterranean, the Caribbean, to give pupils at least a taste of the excitement of contrastive studies? How many teachers who meet immigrant children in their classes are trained to know anything of the language families from which they come? How much professional dialogue is there between teachers of English and those teachers (often untrained) who struggle in difficult conditions to teach their mother tongue to immigrant families who, while desperately wanting and needing English, do not want to lose the language in which their religion and customs are rooted?

Linguistic prejudice
Linguistic prejudices and snobberies which are so endemic in our linguistically naïve community are no longer a joke when they interfere with the life chances of large numbers of children, whether immigrant or any other minority. Prejudice is nurtured by linguistic ignorance and insecurity. It will not be overcome, any more than mistaken notions about the universe or the working of our own bodies will be put right, by leaving it to chance whether pupils pick up the truth incidentally in the course of other studies. The way language works, is acquired, interacts with our thoughts and emotional development, must be studied just as biology must be studied. Of course the study will be conducted, for most pupils, through the medium of the mother tongue as in the other curriculum subjects. But the study of language will go beyond, will get outside, English, and attempt to help the pupil to look objectively at language behaviour, his own included. In this the study will be reinforced by the foreign language element in the curriculum, with which 'language' will be joined in a 'trivium' (English — 'language' — foreign language) planned by a board of studies in each school to form a coherent discipline.

The voters
In our democracy, the voter is often unaware of the influence of the 'hidden persuaders' of the media. Language serves often to obfuscate rather than to inform debate. There is a general naïveté about the relationship of language and thought which leaves the voter vulnerable to the trap of failing to distinguish between concepts which differ because the differences are masked by the linguistic labels attached to them (eg the use of 'immigrant' in Birmingham, or 'loyalist' in Belfast). It is not realistic to suppose that English teaching of the kind that is traditional in our schools will provide the apprenticeship in clear thinking that is needed. It is necessary for the apprentice to distance himself, if only momentarily, from the mother tongue, to turn language in upon itself in an examination of its various uses, of which literary usage may be relatively unimportant. This is not to deny literature a place in the curriculum but to question the wisdom of restricting the study of the use of language in school to literary usage.

The teachers
Evidence of the need for the study of language and thought by teachers is provided by the work of Douglas Barnes and by Coulthard and Sinclair who have listened to dialogue in the classroom. The problem is well described in the paper on language in *Curriculum eleven-sixteen* Working Paper by HM Inspectorate, December 1977:

Anyone, by following a group of pupils through a day in a secondary school, can prove that their language experiences are largely a matter of chance. The dominant modes are exposition by teachers, questions and answers, the writing of notes and answers to work sheets. On any one day, any one of these modes might be dominant.

The pupil's own use of language may be subject to spasmodic correction of superficial features. All of us, to some extent, have a view of language as a mine-field when we have to use it in unfamiliar circumstances. For many pupils, this is especially true; the language of school subjects becomes more and more alien during the years of their secondary education, and they participate less and less in its processes. When they do not understand the characteristics of language in the context of learning, they may fail to develop confidence and incentive to participate that are vital if learning is to take place. We cannot be satisfied with the preparation we give to young people for the language needs of their lives.

Secondary teachers of science, history, art etc are not always sensitive to the demands made on pupils by the language of their different disciplines. Such awareness needs specific training and such training should form part of initial and in-service courses for all teachers. In addition there should be, in every school, teachers who have taken their study of language far enough to be able to supervise the induction of probationers in this asepct of the teacher's craft. It would be the language specialist's responsibility to assemble language teaching materials and keep them up to date, to supervise the language section of the library and to see that language as the central feature of the curriculum had its due allocation of time and resources. This goes far beyond the role of training conventionally given to the teacher of the subject 'English'.

The 'space between' English and other languages

Study of language in the curriculum could be the place where mother-tongue acquisition makes contact with foreign languages and with the languages of immigrants. As it is there is no meeting ground. In most schools teachers of English have no communication at all with foreign language teachers. They read their degrees in separate faculties; they do their training under tutors who seldom meet. Once in post they seldom collaborate, not even to the extent of agreeing to use the same terminology to describe tenses, pronouns, cases etc. Few teachers of English know any other European language at all well. How is this divide to be bridged? Study of language might offer a common meeting ground. English specialists hitherto have shown no awareness even of the need for such a meeting (witness the Bullock Report). The subject 'English' in fact represents one side of the divide that has to be bridged — it can scarcely offer to be the bridge itself.

The Bullock Report *(A language for life* HMSO, 1975)

It was to this failure to give language its due place in the curriculum that many of the most important recommendations of the Bullock Report were directed. The Bullock Report did not in fact accept that language should be a subject in its own right but preferred the solution called 'language across the curriculum' which distributes the onus of language education across all the disciplines. Nevertheless it is hard to see how many of the Bullock proposals could be implemented (eg the proposals regarding the study in the secondary school of young children's acquisition of language) without the creation of a specific curriculum subject: 'Language'.

The decision of the Secretary of State, in 1972, to set up the Committee of Inquiry was itself evidence of anxiety about existing standards in the use of English. The brief accepted by the committee was not limited, as is made clear in the introduction, to standards in reading: '. . . we have, in fact, interpreted our brief as language in education'. The report does not find alarmist allegations of declining standards proven: 'Comparability of levels of literacy between countries is difficult to determine. However, there is no evidence that standards in England are lower than those of other developed countries.' Nevertheless many of the Report's recommendations clearly imply that there are areas of neglect that need remedying. The following are examples:

A substantial course on language in education (including reading) should be part of every primary and secondary school teacher's initial training, whatever the teacher's subject or the age of the children with whom he or she is working. (p. 515)

Parents should be helped to understand the process of language development in their children and play their part in it. (p. 519)

This understanding should begin in the secondary school, where older pupils should be made aware of the adult's role in young children's linguistic and cognitive development. (p. 519)

The study of young children's language by secondary school pupils should wherever possible be firmly based on practical experience in nursery and infant school. (p. 519)

Health and education authorities should cooperate to devise ways of providing expectant parents with advice and information on the language needs of young children. (p. 519)

There should be more opportunities for children to be in a one to one relationship with adults in school.

The additional adults should work in close association with the teacher in helping to carry out the policies she had devised for the children's language development. (p. 520)

In addition to the contribution of nursery nurses and nursery assistants the teacher should have the support of trained 'aides' who have taken a course on language development in the early years. (p. 520)

As part of their professional knowledge teachers should have: an explicit understanding of the processes at work in classroom discourse; the ability to appraise their pupils' spoken language and to plan means of extending it. There should be more opportunities for teachers to study these and other aspects of language in development work and in-service education. (p. 526–7)

In the secondary school, all subject teachers need to be aware of:

(i) the linguistic processes by which their pupils acquire information and understanding, and the implications for the teacher's own use of language;

(ii) the reading demands of their own subjects, and ways in which the pupils
can be helped to meet them. (p. 529)

The thrust of recommendations such as these, taken together, seems certainly to be towards a new dimension for language study both in the school curriculum and in the initial and continuing education of teachers. As to whose responsibility it is going to be to map out and teach this new dimension the Report is unclear. There is a single allusion to linguistics in the recommendations (p. 528):

Linguistics and other specialist studies of language have a considerable contribution to make to the teaching of English, and they should be used to emphasise the inseparability of language and the human situation. Linguistics should not enter schools in the form of the teaching of descriptive grammar.

It is this 'inseparability of language and the human situation' that the committee commends in the programme inititated by Halliday in 1964 under the auspices of the Nuffield Foundation (see Halliday, 1971).

The principle of the programme is to some extent like that of geographical and botanical field work, in that it involves studying 'specimens' of language. These might include the form of the language in which a policeman interviews a witness of an accident, or in which the headlines are written, or in which the meteorologist gives his forecasts.

The Committee, however, is wary of this 'assignments' approach.

Language might come to be seen by some pupils as a series of stereotypes which can be produced to a specification. Unimaginatively used, the programme can become divorced from other aspects of English teaching. (p. 174–5)

On the other hand, at sixth form level, the Committee did take up a proposal (also first made in 1964) (Department of Education and Science, 1964) for the inclusion in the 'A' level GCE examination of a section, as an optional alternative, to cover: 'a study of the structure of the language; the different types of English, dialects and slang; and the relation of language to individual thought and behaviour and also its social implications'.

Having gone quite far along the lines suggested in this paper the Bullock committee proposed the solution they called 'language across the curriculum' which distributes responsibility for language teaching responsibility among all teachers, regardless of specialism. The logical consequence is that all teachers must study language as part of their initial training, and as to how this can be done the Report is clear: ' . . .the best means of ensuring that language is coherently presented is to make it the subject of a separate course' during the Postgraduate Certificate in Education year. No doubt the committee realised how difficult it would be to convince those responsible for teacher training to entertain such a radical notion. Little progress has so far been made in implementing the idea. It deserves the strongest possible support. No teacher ought to be considered a professional without training in language. For the reasons set out in earlier sections of this paper, however, this proposal does not go far enough. The teaching of language is the responsibility of all teachers and all teachers must be trained to play their part. But the subject must have a base in the school, a resource centre, a specialist chiefly responsible for it, otherwise it becomes nobody's responsibility.

Risks of introducing a new curriculum study

Of course it is possible to point to risks in the proposal we are making. A risk facing any proposal for a new element in the curriculum is over-crowding. It was indicated by Eric James, whose colleagues called it 'James's first law of the conservation of the curriculum'. It stated that anyone proposing to add something to the curriculum must be required to say in the same breath what he proposed to leave out to make way for the new element. My reply to that challenge would be: some of the time currently given to English and to a foreign language, because I see the new subject being a link between these two, and being worked out and taught in collaboration by the teachers of English and of the European and ethnic minority languages.

Another possible risk is that some teachers might confuse teaching 'language' with the drilling of correct forms in the belief that cognitive development depends on 'correct' language use, as in some 'remedial' language programmes that linguists have fiercely criticised. There would certainly be real danger in teaching 'language' as a curriculum study unless the teachers had a good grasp of the complexities of the subject. Many college of education students' essays on, for example, the successive Bernstein hypotheses are not reassuring. It is fair for those sceptical of the present proposal to ask, in fact, whether the various schools of research in linguistics and language acquisition have spun out behind them a sufficiently coherent, substantial body of agreed, useful knowledge or shared hypothesis, to constitute a reliable school programme. Some linguists, surveying the present situation of their discipline at undergraduate and graduate level, would prefer to see the rival schools of thought come closer together before trying to devise a school 'language' course. At the same time it is fair to point out that the hazards of superficiality and misunderstanding are increased, not diminished, by the 'language across the curriculum' approach.

A third danger is to misconceive the relationship of language and cognition, and to focus too much attention on the surface patterns of syntax and the extent of vocabulary because they can be perceived, quantified and compared to the neglect of assessment of the precision and complexity of *concepts*, for which we lack parameters and which can only be inferred, often with great difficulty. Yet the interplay of the two 'faces' of the 'concept/label' is constant and subtle, as J.S. Bruner shows (1975):

> This interaction was succinctly put a half-century ago by Sapir (1921) in his *Language*: ' . . .the concept once defined necessarily reacted on the life of its linguistic symbol, encouraging further linguistic growth. We see this complex process of the interaction of language and thought actually taking place under our eyes. The instrument makes possible the product, the products refines the instrument . . . Not until we own the symbol do we feel that we hold a key to the immediate knowledge or understanding of the concept.' For once the symbol is available, it then becomes possible to explore its presuppositional structure, to compile the procedures related to it, to examine the fit between the extended meaning derived linguistically with the experiential tests that can be performed directly on the referent.

67

And earlier in the same essay:

> In assessing the elaborated use of language as a tool of thought, it does not suffice to test for the *presence* in a speech sample of logical, syntactical, or even semantic distinctions, as Labov (1970) has done in order to determine whether non-standard Negro dialect is or is not impoverished. The issue, rather, is how language is being used, what in fact the subject is *doing* with his language.

Recent work in language acquisition (cf. Halliday's *Learning how to mean*) and in English in school (Wight's *Concept seven-nine*) reminds us of the complexity of the concept/language relationship.

What it might look like

Despite the admitted risks, the shortcomings of the present curriculum, except for children from highly articulate home backgrounds, are so obvious that we must be prepared to make a trial at least. What would teachers need to know? The Bullock Report devoted considerable space to proposals for initial and in-service training courses in language. Two examples of a basic language course for teachers are printed in an appendix to the Bullock Report. The following paragraphs attempt to sketch a brief outline of a course in 'language' at the three levels: junior, secondary and sixth form. The elements proposed should be thought of as *additional* to the 'learning how to mean' which already figures in imaginative English courses.

Junior level

In the first school and the first two years of middle school (ie up to the age of eleven years) the study might include the following elements, worked out cooperatively by teachers of the mother tongue, of music and of a foreign language:

(i) Education of the ear — progressive training in discrimination and explorations of rhythms, tunes, intonation patterns, varieties of English accents. Children need to learn to hear just as they need to learn to see. It is a longer and harder lesson, partly because shortterm memory capacity imposes severe restraints for many children on the amount of the information they can take in via the ear and on their capacity to 'process' incoming aural messages. Learning via the eye poses fewer problems for children whose STM capacity is limited.

(ii) Exploration of sounds (and songs) of the languages of our neighbours, to awaken curiosity and give confidence in meeting different languages. This would include, in areas with ethnic minorities, planned, serious listening to each other's speech sounds and songs, by children from the various ethnic groups in the school population, learning to count in each other's languages etc.

(iii) Setting up expectations about language, since learning depends so much on the fulfilling of expectations. To take a simple example, children might be prepared fairly systematically to *expect* surface ambiguities in language use, and to become familiar with different kinds of verbal ambiguity (eg, through riddles and puns etc).

(iv) Above all the junior school course must support children whose homes have not helped them to develop what Margaret Donaldson (1978) calls 'awareness' of language. This is the ability to disentangle language which is 'embedded' in its context, in its associations with persons and places, from the non-linguistic signals which are so important for the child. On this awareness of purely linguistic signals depends the child's ability to learn in school and to make the breakthrough to literacy on which all the rest of his verbal education is going to depend.

Secondary level

In the secondary school (post eleven-plus) there would be a largely project-based study of language in society to include practical work on language acquisition, as well as on language differences, dialects, registers, prejudices etc. based on critical listening to tape recording and to television and radio. History of language would be introduced, illustrated by place names. (An imaginative syllabus is worked out in eg B.N. Ball, *Basic linguistics for secondary schools*, 1966.)

In the sixth form the Bullock Report's endorsement of the SSEC (1964) recommendation of a language option at 'A' level, might be taken as a starting point. However the first step would be to develop a new 'N' level language paper on offer to all sixth formers regardless of their specialism. The sixth form study of language might well assume something like the role that used to be claimed for *philosophie* in the Baccalauréat. It could be the element in the curriculum which brought together in regular discussion not only the pupils whose specialisms normally kept them apart, but their teachers too.

The above outline is deliberately tentative and short; discussion by working parties of practising teachers together with teacher trainers will greatly improve it. It should be read as *supplementing* the Bullock proposals for teachers' language courses and such admirable schemes as *Concept seven-nine* etc.

The meeting place for L1 and L2

To summarise: we are arguing for a coherent approach to language as the discipline underlying the rest of the curriculum. Essentially the case for the study of language as a separate subject is that it would equip pupils better to learn both their mother tongue and a foreign language and that it would provide an ideal meeting place for the two subjects which are at present studied in isolation. As we have seen, one of the most surprising aspects of *A Language for Life* was the complete absence, throughout its 600 pages, of any recognition that the pupils concerned are going to live their lives in ever closer contact with their neighbours who speak interestingly different languages. Even more revealing is that it was not felt necessary to offer any explanation for such insularity. Language 'across the curriculum' turned out to mean 'part-way across the curriculum'. We are arguing for 'language at the centre of the curriculum'. Not the least of the attractions of the kind of study proposed in this paper is that it could serve as a unifying discipline in the curriculum, not only for native-English speaking children but for the minority children in Britain too. There are two kinds of insularity in Britain — (a) Britons versus foreigners, including the EEC! and (b) Britons versus the immigrants. Schools where the study of language, on the lines suggested above, might be most beneficial are those with a proportion of non-English speakers. It will be clear that the subject 'language' so conceived is very far from being simply a widening of the conventional study of English. What is proposed is a subject that will be a bridge across the 'space between' English and the rest. The Bullock Committee's proposals, despite their insights and imaginative encouragement to teachers, fail to meet the reality of the polyglot world in which our children will grow up and of the multi-cultural cities in which they must learn to welcome and value diversity in language as in much else. Moreover the Bullock Committee's own proposals to involve all teachers in responsibility for language across the curriculum can only be successful if there is one subject area with a specially trained teacher of language in charge of it, to serve as a nucleus to which all teachers can refer for guidance, materials and encouragement.

References

Aitchison, J. *The articulate mammal: an introduction to psycholinguistics.* Hutchinson, 1976.

Bruner, J.S. 'Language as an instrument of thought.' In *Problems of language and learning.* Edited by A. Davies. Heinemann Educational, 1975.

Committee of Inquiry into Reading and the Use of English. *A Language for life.* HMSO, 1975. (The Bullock Report.)

Department of Education and Science. *The examining of English language.* 8th report of the Secondary Schools Examinations Council. HMSO, 1964.

Donaldson, M. *Children's minds.* Fontana, 1978.

Halliday, M.A.K. Foreword to *Language in use*, by P. Doughty, J. Pearce and G. Thornton. Edward Arnold, 1971.

Halliday, M.A.K. *Learning how to mean: explorations in the development of language.* Edward Arnold, 1975.

HM Inspectorate of Schools. *Curriculum 11–16: a contribution to current debate, December 1977.* Department of Education and Science, 1978.

Saussure, F. *Cours de linguistique générale.* 1915.

Schools Council. *Concept seven-nine.* Prepared by Schools Council Project based at Birmingham University. E.J. Arnold for Schools Council, 1973.

Smith, G. ed. *The West Riding Project.* Educational priority: report of a research project sponsored by the Department of Education and Science and the Social Science Research Council, vol 4. HMSO, 1975.

5. Mother tongue and foreign language teaching in France

C.E. Dawson

This chapter attempts to examine what seems to be the main aims and objectives of the teaching of French and of English (far and away the predominant foreign language taught) in France. Highly centralised though the national educational system is, however, no short and clear-cut presentation is possible. This is firstly because France, in common with so many western countries, is undergoing a period of far-reaching cultural change, and shifting values readily make their effects felt in educational affairs. Secondly, the official position as represented by the Ministry of Education is the subject for widespread and often passionate debate and disagreement. Teachers continue as always to accept, or to interpret, or indeed largely to ignore, the policy and the sometimes quite detailed guidelines contained in the *Instructions* and other governmental documents. Finally, of course, it is hardly satisfactory to stop at 'aims' without at least a glance at the practical consequences in terms of methods of work, teaching materials, and assessment procedures.

An observer from Britain may well be struck initially by the fact that the French, whether as individuals, in groupings, or on the national level, take for granted the need to begin with a consideration of aims and principles, whereas a less articulate, more pragmatic, approach may leave so much unsaid that compromise and adjustment are not difficult to achieve. The French habit of spelling out a position, of offering a text for public discussion and so often rejection, seems to produce not the hoped-for consensus, but a situation of permanent conflict. Education in France has invariably been subject to the bitterest of partisan controversy, and clearly, where language teaching is concerned there are immediate ideological complications, especially in view of the current moves towards *démocratisation* and an *enseignement de masse*. The present brief account can hardly aspire to reflect the light and shade of this complex situation.

With regard, first, to the teaching of the mother tongue, it is convenient to start by referring to recent changes, but with the caveat that old-established attitudes and practices are still to be found. There is ample evidence of regret for the passing of the older approach to the teaching of (an un-questioned) 'correct' French, with its emphasis on spelling, dictation, traditional rules of grammar, and the model presented by the great writers. Though obviously a caricature, the admonition *'écris et tais-toi'* has been taken to sum up this approach: the written form was utterly dominant, and where oral work occurred it was normally in the form of *récitation* or *élocution* using literary texts. However, France like other countries entered a rather more child-centred phase, (with certain typically French features — one thinks, for example, of Freinet), which placed emphasis less on *la norme scolaire* than on the pupil's spontaneous effort. Currently, both these trends may be seen alongside the growing

71

influence of linguistic studies of some awareness of psycho- and socio-linguistic considerations (though the latter appear to be slower to affect French attitudes, and especially the content of teacher-training courses). Characteristically, the teaching of grammar is not in question, however acrimonious the debate on 'which grammar?' and 'how?'. But now the main concern is with *communication*, with language as an effective means of self-expression in a social context. Lest this may seem to be a simple echo of an Anglo-American approach, it should be noted that the refinement of the language tool, and conscious reflection upon its nature and function, are constantly emphasised. We see here a partial not complete rejection of the traditional accent upon analysis; a lively debate continues on the question of grammatical terminology (the official *Nomenclature grammaticale* issued in 1975 is hotly contested by the linguists) and on the teaching of a metalanguage which would enable the older pupil to develop his understanding of the language he uses. Old-style labelling, and parsing and analysis, have in any case largely succumbed to the onslaught of the linguists — the structuralist school and more recently Chomskian transformational ideas have already had a marked impact on published courses in French for both primary and secondary pupils. Indeed the use of structural exercises, comparable to those used for FL teaching in the UK, figures quite prominently in course-books for the mother tongue. One extreme technique, the presentation of the sentence by means of a tree-diagram, has been tried and by many rejected in the last year or two. Perhaps most frequent and more promising is the thematic approach, whereby a topic is chosen (often by the pupils themselves) which takes into consideration, in addition to purely linguistic objectives, pupil-participation and cooperation, supported by team-teaching and audio-visual as well as purely text-based material. In this latter connection also, language teaching is seen in a wider educational context. In France, as in England, a movement is perceptible towards interdisciplinary work and a sense of language across the curriculum; typically, the theoretical bases are much discussed, and the distinction is made between inter-, pluri-, and multi-disciplinary approaches. But for the outside observer so much depends upon which school and indeed which classroom one finds oneself in: a class of fifteen/sixteen year olds studying Zola's novel *L'Assommoir* by means of a strip cartoon of their own creation — or a class of ten year olds acquiring the term *phonème* as part of a systematic study of the correlation of sound and spelling.

In attempting to sum up the overall aims of the teaching of French in France, it is tempting to be satisfied with an account of documents emanating from official committees, and of recent Ministerial circulars. Clearly these are evidence of a very significant nature: among the former, the *Plan Rouchette* (1971) which has influenced language work in the primary school, and the report of the *Commission Emmanuel* (1975) for the secondary stage. Both have called for a thorough review of objectives and teaching-styles, indeed for reform and *rénovation* in these areas, but alongside *libération* Rouchette maintains a characteristic demand for *structuration*, whilst Emmanuel (himself, by the way, neither civil servant nor teacher, but a poet of some stature), or rather his eight working-parties, survey every aspect of their vast subject before making practical suggestions for change. An important preoccupation is that of diagnosing and making good the social handicap suffered by the child with inadequate language. But this encyclopaedic Report concerns itself too with the impact of linguistics on the French lesson, with literature (but as only one aspect of the linguistic side of culture) . . . and, recognising that aims cannot be achieved in the absence of suitable teacher training, includes a section proposing a far more comprehensive and practical approach to this problem than is at present the case.

What is striking about teacher-training as it exists at present in France, is the minimal attention given to the professional (as opposed to the academic) preparation provided for the top-flight. In the markedly hierarchical structure of the profession, these are the teachers succeeding, after the university, in the fiercely competitive state-examinations for the *Agrégation* and the CAPES (*Certificate d'aptitude péda-gogique a l'enseignement secondaire*). For the former there is almost no professional preparation, and they will expect to teach in the sixteen-plus, *Lycée* or the university faculty. The latter, (somewhat lower on the scale of status and qualification — and having to teach more hours weekly) will have, in addition to excellent command of their subject, a year's course in which their time is divided between study, under the guidance of *conseillers pédagogiques*, at a Regional Pedagogical Centre (CPR) and three short periods of teaching practice. For both groups however the preparation is heavily criticised by French educationists as out-of-date and largely out of touch with present needs. In fact, it is the future primary and twelve to sixteen college teachers, trained in the departmental training colleges, who benefit from the most adequate professional courses. There are fewer foreign-language teachers in this category, but many teachers of the mother tongue, and a strong linguistic element is evident in the syllabus they follow. At least it may be said that the French (like ourselves?) are striving to see not just the isolated problems of their educational provision, but the 'problematic' of the whole, of which language study is a pervasive and determining element. However, to a greater extent than ourselves (at least, up to present) they relate any expression of principle or of aim to a broader philosophical and political position, thus making it more difficult to attain that minimal consensus required for agreement on matters of practice.

This can be seen at once in the promulgation of the *Instructions officielles* and the issue of less binding guidelines through the *Courrier de l'Education*. The very comprehensive *Instructions* of 1972 relating to the teaching of French in the primary school (*Ecole elémentaire*) might seem to be admirable reflections of recent pro-gressive thinking: to some however such official pronouncements are a betrayal of the best in the French cultural tradition, to others they represent *la pédagogie étatique*, an unworthy compromise by which the Government ensures the survival of social selection by means of the education system (and in particular by the way in which French is taught); the State is accused both of denying the proper resources to its schools, and conspiring in the maintenance of an unjust political and social system. Several of the teachers' unions are loud and articulate in this debate. For example, in 1977 the Ministerial circular spoke of correct spelling as 'a social necessity' while a manifesto of the AFEF (L'Association Française des Enseignants de Français) described it as a 'social myth'. A point of especial interest to the foreign observer nonetheless is the frequency and vehemence with which one fundamental argument is forthcoming: it is not in the interests of the socially underprivileged child for the teacher to meet him on his own cultural ground, and in the language of his own family and street; rather, such a child should be offered the challenge, and brought up in the use of a socially acceptable language by which he will be able later to assert himself. Language is power, and language is a means whereby the learner may accede to that state of *autonomie* (a basic tenet of current educational thinking in France) which means full and equal citizenship. Equally, the French seem never to have lost sight of the intellectual and the cognitive aspect of mother-tongue learning, as a vital part of the education of all pupils. It is ironical to recall the extent to which a more behaviouristic approach was adopted for the early stages of the French-produced course in French for foreigners (*Voix et Images de France* CREDIF, 1963 onwards). This trend is now much questioned.

To end with a specific statement on 'aims' we need simply to turn to the *Courrier de l'Education* no 49, April 1977. Here in six or seven hundred words we find the official position regarding the aims of the teaching of French in the twelve to sixteen comprehensive college: clear and intelligible speech; the ability to contribute coherently to a discussion, to communicate information and ideas effectively and with due regard to style, register and audience; the ability to read with ease and understanding, to assess and comment upon a wide range of current reading material; some acquaintance with longer written works of eg literary, documentatary or scientific interest, and with a variety of styles. In addition the pupil shall learn to seek out, classify, and use different kinds of information, and to handle card-indexes and filing-systems. He shall be able to make notes, write reports, and carry out day-to-day language-tasks (eg send a telegram); he shall have some appreciation of language as a vehicle for the logical expression of ideas. Attention will be given to legibility of handwriting, accuracy of spelling and correctness of grammar, and the pupil will be familiar with the use of dictionaries, have some knowledge of word-formation and of grammatical terminology and rules. He will have read, and *studied* in class (the word used is *expliqué*) extracts and works representing the French literary heritage of the past and present, and will have learned a number of poems by heart.

It may be of interest, in turning to the aims of foreign language teaching, to compare with this brief but explicit statement the corresponding programme for the first foreign language (*Courrier de l'Education* of the same date, but also an issue of earlier date (Feb 1977, no 45) specially devoted to modern languages). The move to a functional and utilitarian approach is clear (it is recalled that this refers to the age-group in the twelve to sixteen comprehensive school — a note upon the aims for students of sixteen-plus will occur later in this paper). The foreign language programme is presented in three stages (*niveaux*), the first two of which correspond to the two cycles of the *collège* ie twelve to fourteen (*observation*) and fourteen to sixteen (*orientation*). *Niveau 3* takes place in the sixteen-plus *lycées*, new style.

In issue no 49 of the *Courrier*, something over 1000 words are devoted to the aims of teaching the first foreign language, with a section each for grammar, vocabulary, and the four major skills. The emphasis is laid upon ability to communicate in the language, together with adequate knowledge of the foreign country and its ways. Functional grammar is to be taught through the presentation of authentic language in a situation, and learned by practice and use. Basic structures of statement, question, etc are listed, and include complex as well as simple forms; notional items are also included: modal verbs, expression of basic concepts such as quantity, degree, frequency, causation, consequence, intention, hypothesis etc. An active and functional vocabulary of 1200 to 1400 words is suggested, with passive/recognition vocabulary in addition. Topics to be covered are of the everyday kind, though a footnote does refer to brief and elementary information on political, economic and social matters. The learner should be able to express personal opinions, and various emotional states, including agreement and disagreement. A degree of organisation and conceptualisation should be progressively developed, so that the young learner is able to make maximum use of his 'competence' in correct 'performance' (these Chomskian terms are quoted from the text). The pupil must be trained and psychologically prepared to extract global and general meaning from what he hears; his oral command should include an acceptable pronunciation, eschewing 'perfectionism', and an ability to express himself effectively in a real (or in classroom terms, realistic) situation; in reading, he should be able to manage more complex structures and a more sustained line of narrative or reasoning; writing skills should include correct spelling and sentence construction, in the form of narrative *résumé*, and a letter. There is finally a tentative reference to the possibility of translation work, from the FL into French.

This succinct programme of current requirements is put into a broader perspective by the article in *Courrier* no 45 which recalls the earlier cultural/intellectual approach to FL teaching in the secondary school. It does not reject, but rather adds to, the earlier position — the dimension of language for communication in the context of international contact and understanding. It thus stresses the functional aspect, especially in the early years of secondary education, when the teaching must be as concrete and the learning as active as possible. The emphasis will be on oral work, with 'thinking about grammar' arising only as the pupils show the necessary maturity. The FL must be firmly set in an appropriate background of civilisation and culture if it is fully to contribute to a sound humanistic education. The pupil must be lead beyond the stage of purely instrumental use of the language as a series of mechanically acquired skills — the major objective of the audio-visual approach of the sixties. Now teachers are urged to cultivate in their pupils critical observation, and a thoughtful, reasoned, approach to the language they are learning. The teacher, essential though his role is seen to be, is there to stimulate and organise the activity of his class but not to dominate in the unilateral style of some years ago. The ideal remains the *bain de langue* though without the doctrinaire exclusion of any word of the mother tongue. As for grammar, it should not be taught by means of rules, but *la réflexion grammaticale* should 'arise inductively from actual use of the foreign language' . . . there is no further advice on this perennially difficult point, merely a call for constant flexibility, which takes into account the psychological needs of the learner . . . Regarding the proper attitude towards learners' errors, here again: flexibility. Self-and reciprocal-correction by pupils is recommended, in addition to continuous evaluation by the teacher. There is no reference to the requirement — in some schools — that marks be supplied for administrative purposes, but there is a remark upon the enormous discretion left to the individual teacher . . . and the responsibility placed upon him to provide suitably for all his charges, whether they are soon to leave school for employment or to continue language study either for general interest or specialist purposes.

It was no part of the document just considered to deal with the problems of the post-sixteen pupil, though some reference to building up grammatical understanding was made, as was a reference to the steady development of written skills. The so-called *Niveau 3* however is receiving much attention in France at the moment. Indeed, the *choc en retour* (or backwash effect) exercised by each successive stage on the preceding ones has already begun to have a most beneficial effect. Thus (as suggested above) the rather behaviouristic procedures often adopted in the first two years, in order to inculcate linguistic *automatismes* and regardless of pupils' reaction and motivation, have been much modified by the closer attention given to learning-objectives and psychological factors in stage 2: a general move towards greater autonomy and self-expression on the part of the pupil is occurring. Similarly, one reads in an issue of *Les Amis de Sèvres* (March 1978), entitled *Langues Vivantes: Niveau 3*, of changing aims and practices which are finding, or will certainly find, their echo at lower levels. The clear call is for foreign-language teaching which will contribute to the general education, the growing maturity, and the personal *autonomy* of the individual, whilst at the same time providing him with a language experience which has relevance to the modern world, and can be put to whatever use he may subsequently require. But the new-style *lycées*, recruiting at sixteen those who wish to continue their school education beyond the statutory limit, are being obliged to develop new methods if their acknowledged aims are to be achieved with the surprisingly heterogeneous pupils they receive from the *collèges*. Heterogeneous, that is to say, in respect of their interests and needs (factors not given the highest priority) and with regard to levels of attainment and linguistic ability. In his introduction to the Sèvres pamphlet, M. l'Inspecteur Général Denis Girard indicates some of the solutions which are being proposed and tested. These include a flexible grouping of classes, whose FL teachers work together in a team; in this way allowance can be made for broad-banded ability grouping on particular occasions, thus permitting each group to do some of its work at a different pace and with a 'differentiated pedagogy' from the others, whilst avoiding the worst effects of blatant streaming. The need to make an initial decision on each pupil's placing has made it essential to devise suitable diagnostic tests for incoming students. A precondition of such an approach is the ability and willingness of colleagues to work together — the importance of such *concertation* is increasingly stressed. Among the vital questions to which a team of teachers has to address itself is the choice of course-book and other material, and still more important, their adaptation to the particular needs of the pupils. In fact, at this level a good deal of material is of the non-didactic kind, chosen from newspapers and periodicals with a view to appealing directly to the interests of the students and avoiding the artificialty of the specially created text. The aim then is to help the learners to formulate genuinely personal reactions and ideas of their own, as a development of the more limited and imitative expression associated with an earlier stage of learning.

Since it is universally recognised that in any system the nature of external examinations will inevitably exert an influence for good or ill on the way in which teachers teach and learners learn, a brief word needs to be said about the *Baccalauréat* examination. With increasing reliance upon internal assessment and teachers' reports, this state examination taken at age eighteen or nineteen has in effect become the only external examination now operating in the French school system. Though the particular 'bac' which he sits will vary according to the student's choice of course (eg with an emphasis on languages, economics, maths/physics etc) he will take a compulsory oral examination as well as a written test in French, and also a compulsory oral examination in a foreign language (in which he may also take a written test). It is the oral examinations which seem to cause the greatest dissatisfaction among teachers: not only are they considered to be far too cursory (and may constitute the only end-of-course foreign-language test taken by the candidate) but since this is a requirement of all candidates whatever their special subject interest, the pass level is regarded as much too low. In the mother tongue, the oral normally involves the candidate in conversation upon one of a list of twenty or more texts, or topics of a less literary kind, which he has recently studied. For a foreign language, in the fifteen minutes or so available, the examiner is attempting to assess a daunting number of different kinds of knowledge and skill. Many question the validity of the test, and would wish to see a more substantial and better designed oral examination as the culmination of a course in which oral communication is given such high priority. M.P. Moreau, in the Sèvres document already quoted, calls for serious reconsideration of both oral and written tests of FL in the *Baccalauréat*, seeing them realistically as 'both carrot and stick', but as failing either to test adequately or to motivate in the way that they might. Teachers of French can be heard expressing themselves in similar vein: the 'oral' is too often a somewhat inconsequential conversation, the prepared material providing no basis for satisfactory assessment; whilst the four-hour written examination has the merit of offering choice between the literary dissertation, the general dissertation, and the résumé, it again fails to reflect the teaching programmes or to exert upon them a coherent and beneficial backwash effect.

Recent changes and the continuing vigorous debate give promise that attempts to reform and renovate will produce further progress. The work of the *collèges expérimentaux*, for example, and the regular conferences held for inspectors and teachers at the Centre International d'Etudes Pédagogiques near Paris, as well as at provincial centres, ensure that the questioning and innovative spirit is kept alive, and that some *généralisation* of the best thinking and practice can take place.

Finally, an aspect of the question which is of particular interest to the National Congress on Languages in Education, viz the relationship between the learning and teaching of the mother tongue and of a foreign language, remains to be mentioned. In the course of pluridisciplinary team-teaching, there are occasions when a common topic is treated by both mother-tongue and foreign language teachers. Though sometimes labelled *interdisciplinarité*, it is clear that there is rather a certain parallelism than any degree of interrelationship between the two partners in this approach. At another level however there may be signs of recognized common ground — this is in the teaching of grammar, and the introduction of concepts and terminology involving the acquisition, by those pupils who are able, of a so-called metalanguage with which to aid that *réflexion sur la langue* to which reference is so often made

77

in French education. It is clear too, that such thinking is having its effect at various levels of teacher training, as more and more often basic texts on general linguistics are brought into use. As to the application of these ideas in terms of day-to-day classroom teaching, it seems that in France as in the UK, a comprehensive didactic theory has still to be developed.

References

Les Amis de Sèvres. Nos 85 and 89, CIEP, Sèvres, 1978.
Aujourd 'hui le Français. (Manifesto of the Association Française des Enseignants de Français, 1977).
Circulaires, Instructions, and *Programmes* of the French Ministry of Education.
Courrier de l'Education. Nos 45 and 49, the French Ministry of Education, 1977.
Pour une Réforme de l'Enseignement du Français. (Commission Emmanuel.) INRDP, Paris 1975.
Recherches Pédagogiques. No 47 (Plan Rouchette), INRDP, Paris 1971.
Also articles in *Le Français dans le Monde, Langue Française, L'Ecole Libératrice, L'Ecole et la Nation, Le Monde de l'Education.*

The writer would like to express particular thanks to the Director of the Centre International d'Etudes Pédagogiques at Sèvres, and to his colleagues, for the help and documentation which they provided.

6. Mother-tongue and foreign-language assessment in North America

In North America, there has been an increasing acceptance over the past ten years or so that some form of accountability in education is inevitable. As in this country, there has been considerable public debate about the vexed issue of 'standards' in education — usually with the gut feeling that things aren't what they used to be — and the idea has steadily gained ground that schools are accountable to society for the use to which they put their resources and the success with which they achieve their objectives. Many of the individual states and provinces now carry out regular broadscale programmes of student assessment, although these tend to be restricted to a fairly limited range of basic skills and, in the main, rely heavily on the use of multiple-choice tests, whether commercially available or developed in response to specific local requirements.

In addition, in the United States alone, the assessment of student performance in certain areas of the school curriculum has been undertaken on a national basis under the auspices of the National Assessment of Educational Progress (NAEP) each year for the past nine years. Interestingly, although the NAEP programme devotes a considerable amount of its resources to the testing of various aspects of proficiency in the English language and, indeed, ranges quite widely over the school curriculum, it makes no provision whatsoever for testing student performance in any foreign language. This is, in general, equally true of the individual state assessment programmes: the emphasis normally falls heavily on the assessment of basic skills which, in the language context, has tended to emerge as a concentration on the assessment of such English reading skills as are amenable to large-scale multiple-choice testing. Until recently, there have been few attempts to assess students' writing skills in any direct manner and even fewer to assess their listening and speaking skills.

In the United States, at least, this has been largely because the state assessment programmes have tended to be linked, explicitly or implicitly, with a rather limited notion of educational accountability. In its most extreme form, this type of programme has been limited to basic skill assessment and has involved the 'blanket' testing of all students in given school grades, usually by means of standardised multiple-choice tests. The best-known example of this approach is probably that of the Michigan Educational Assessment Programme, which is based on the measurement of 'minimal' performance objectives in certain basic skill areas, notably mathematics and reading. This programme has aroused considerable controversy, both within the United States and abroad. From the outset, much bitterness and hostility was kindled among the teaching force in Michigan when the state educational authorities were pressured by politicians into releasing the test results for individual schools, having previously assured the teachers concerned that these would remain confidential to local school administrators. The test results were actually published in local newspapers, giving rise to a 'league table' of schools (apparently much in demand among the estate agents of the area), which took no account of the schools' differing human and financial resources. Teachers complained bitterly that the tests used in the assessment programme did not adequately reflect the school curriculum, that there had been little or no teacher involvement in the development of the tests, and that the concept of 'minimal' performance objectives was both nebulous and potentially stifling to all but the least able of students.

The debate spread beyond Michigan and grew even more heated when it was announced in 1971 that a new compensatory education programme (*Chapter 3*) would tie the distribution of federal funds to the Michigan achievement test results. This was to be done by arranging for those school districts with the highest number of low-achieving students to be funded first, then those with lower numbers, until the available funds were exhausted. Once the money reached the school districts, the lowest-achieving students were to be identified on the basis of local test scores: those selected were to remain in the programme for three years. Each school district was required to specify its own performance objectives: the most common response was to specify one month's academic growth for each month in the programme, as measured by locally-chosen standardised tests.

Funds for the second year of the programme were to be allocated according to the first year's test results: for each student achieving 75 per cent of the specified objectives, the school district would receive a full per-student allocation for the next year; for each student achieving less than 75 per cent of the specified objectives, the school district was to receive a lesser amount, proportionate to the gains achieved. In the event, it proved impossible to implement this policy for the first year of the programme and, in 1972, *Chapter 3* was amended by the inclusion of a first-year waiver. The law continued to stipulate, however, that the achievement test results for the second year would determine the allocation of funds for the third year of the programme. In fact, when the 1972–1973 test results became available, it was revealed that more than a third of the *Chapter 3* students had fallen short of the 75 per cent goal, entailing a potential loss of five million dollars if the incentive provision were to be implemented. Again, there was intensive local lobbying to have the incentive provision waived and, again, the state education authorities and the legislature yielded to the pressure. The situation apparently remains unchanged today. As far as one can tell, the incentive provision has not been implemented: funds have not been withheld from the low-scoring school districts. Nevertheless, the whole episode has left an aftermath of resentment among the teachers involved and a lingering belief that the attitude of the state education authority towards the teaching profession is a punitive rather than a supportive one, placing an undue emphasis on minimal student achievement within a narrow band of competencies.

A less controversial version of this approach to assessment, again with an emphasis on the measurement of basic literacy and numeracy skills, can be seen in operation in California, where all students in given school grades are tested, but the same tests are not administered to all students. Instead, the technique of matrix sampling is employed, the test items covering a given area of the curriculum being divided into a number of sub-sets and each sub-set being given to a different group of students. In this way, a group of ten students, each responding to a different sub-set of test items within a 30-minute period, can provide test data comparable to, or even superior to, that provided by one student subjected to five hours' testing.

The use of this technique greatly lessens the impact of a programme of assessment on the life of an individual school and, in addition, eliminates the distorting factor of student fatigue. Since the students in any one school are likely to receive different sub-sets of items, the temptation to 'teach to the test' is also reduced to a minimum.

The Californian approach generates information about the overall performance of students in the state as a whole, in individual school systems and in individual schools, but it cannot generate information relating to particular classes or teachers: the smallest 'accountable' unit is thus the whole school, not the individual teacher. In addition, the Californian schools are compared not solely in terms of their students' absolute performance, but also in terms of the relative performance of their students when compared with that found in schools in similar circumstances, with an intake similar in ability, socio-economic status, language background and mobility rate. After the administration of the tests, each school receives computer print-out showing the mean score for the school compared with those for the school district, the state, and the nation as a whole. The school's overall performance is given a rank score and is shown in comparison with the range of performance achieved in schools in similar circumstances. This procedure is clearly more defensible than one in which schools are compared directly, without regard to the varying circumstances in which they operate and the differing human and financial resources available to them.

The technique of matrix sampling, but applied this time to a national probability sample, is also a feature of the NAEP approach to assessment and is undoubtedly one of the reasons why NAEP has managed to avoid antagonising the American teaching profession. The NAEP assessment programme is not concerned with individual schools, teachers or students, but seeks to describe the performance of representative groups of students and to document changes in national standards of performance over time. Another factor which might well have helped to increase the acceptability of the NAEP programme has been the extensive involvement, from the early planning stages onwards, of practising teachers and their union representatives in the design and development of the programme. One of the criticisms most frequently levelled at the statewide assessment programmes is the lack of teacher involvement in the setting-up of the programmes and in the development of the tests used to implement them. Most of the state assessment programmes are based on the use of commercially-available standardised tests, or on apparently similar ones developed locally: as already noted, these tend to concentrate heavily on the measurement of basic skills, sometimes with the addition of 'basic life competencies'. Many of them seem strangely divorced from the realities of the classroom and are justifiably regarded by the teachers concerned as an inadequate basis for the assessment of their students' achievements. It is not unusual for example, to encounter 'writing' tests which do not require the student to write at all — merely to place ticks in boxes — and 'mathematics' tests whose reading load far exceeds their mathematical content. The details of how these tests were developed are rarely available for public scrutiny and the tests themselves are usually closely protected by stringent security restrictions. In this connection, the NAEP programme stands out as a shining example: from the outset, it has maintained a massive and well-documented test development effort, making a genuine and sustained attempt to break away from the more traditional and circumscribed means of assessment, and, on each occasion of testing, has released 50 per cent of the items for local use. This latter policy is beginning to have a considerable impact on the state assessment programmes, particularly in areas, such as writing, where the assessment of student performance has traditionally been very limited in its scope and nature.

Whatever the shortcomings of the NAEP approach to assessment, its test programme has a breadth and an originality rarely found in the individual state enterprises. This is nowhere more apparent than in the assessment of students' expressive writing, an area of performance notable by its absence from most state endeavours. The NAEP approach includes asking students to express their feelings in writing on listening to a piece of music such as Scott Joplin's *New rag*, to take part in an imaginative situation, such as pretending to live the life of a pair of tennis shoes, to respond in writing to a complex picture, to write a personal letter of thanks, compassion, persuasion or complaint, to respond in writing to a telephone conversation, or to write a letter answering an advertisement, rectifying an error, or applying for a job.

The NAEP assessment of reading skills was, initially at least, far less innovative than its assessment of writing skills. The early NAEP reading test items were arranged in so-called 'clusters', which were meant to provide meaningful 'themes' for reporting purposes. These 'themes' bore such titles as 'understanding words and word relationships', 'gleaning significant facts from passages', 'drawing inferences', and so on. The same stimulus material, but with a different question attached to it, was used to illustrate more than one theme. For instance, in the early reading tests, (NAEP, 1971) the following passage, amongst others, appeared several times:

The wind pushed the boat farther and farther out to sea. It started to rain and the fog grew thick. The boy and his father were lost at sea.

When accompanied by the instruction to complete the following response:

The weather was:
- (a) calm
- (b) dry
- (c) sunny
- (d) wet
- (e) I don't know

it was used to illustrate the theme 'gleaning significant facts from passages'. When the response to be completed was:

This story is MAINLY about:
- (a) the wind
- (b) fun at the seashore
- (c) a ride in a new car
- (d) I don't know

the exercise illustrated the theme 'main ideas and organisation'. Appearing again with the following question:

At least how many people were in the boat?

    (a) One
    (b) two
    (c) three
    (d) four
    (e) five
    (f) I don't know

the exercise was used to illustrate the theme 'drawing inferences'. And so on.

Although this thematic approach helped to give some organisation to the presentation of the test results, it must be admitted that the attachment of a given item to a particular 'theme' often had a somewhat unconvincingly *post hoc* air about it. Another drawback was that the results were presented item by item, which gave a very staccato impression of the findings and left the reader with the difficult task of trying to form an overall view of the results from a mass of disparate and highly detailed fragments of information. The value of the information that can be derived from this type of presentation is also, of course, heavily dependent on the quality of the individual items: many of the early NAEP reading items, particularly those cast in the multiple-choice format, were castigated as inadequate to bear the weight of individual statistical analysis. In fairness to NAEP, however, it must be said that the new generation of reading test items, not yet publicly available, looks far more promising and innovative than its predecessor.

Recently, NAEP has turned its attention to investigating the feasibility of testing listening and speaking skills on a national basis but, so far, they have not managed to proceed beyond indirect forms of assessment, as when, for example, a student is asked to judge how appropriate given responses are in a particular set of circumstances. An example of this type of item is given below:

You have been selected to host the awards ceremony for the Glendale Junior Service Club. Which would be the best way to introduce the winner of the outstanding volunteer award?

1. 'We all know Nancy. She's been a member of the club for three years now. She's a great kid. Nancy, come up and get the outstanding volunteer award.'

2. 'The outstanding volunteer award is given each year to the club member who demonstrated exceptional service and enthusiasm in club activities. This year's award goes to Nancy Joyce for her excellent job organising this year's newspaper drive. Congratulations, Nancy.'

3. 'This evening we wish to recognise Miss Nancy Joyce for her noteworthy service in the Glendale Junior Service Club. She was responsible for directing this year's successful newspaper drive. For this we present her with the outstanding volunteer award.'

4. 'I don't know.'

At the end of the awards ceremony which of the following statements would be the best way for you to conclude the presentation?

1. 'This concludes the Ninth Annual Glendale Junior Service Club Awards Ceremony. It has been a great honour for me to be a part of this important occasion.'
2. 'That's it. We have had a super year. I hope the next will be just as great.'
3. 'This marks the end of another year for the Glendale Junior Service Club. We can look back at our accomplishments with pride and look forward to another productive and fun-filled year.'
4. 'I don't know.' (Mead, 1977)

It must be emphasised, however, that this is a relatively new venture and that NAEP's plans for assessment in the area of speaking and listening skills are far more comprehensive than the test items to appear so far would suggest, as the list of objectives for the new assessment programme, given in the appendix, clearly indicates.

Canada has no national assessment programme analogous to that operating in the United States: the largest unit of assessment is that of the individual province. Most provinces undertake some form of regular assessment of student performance but, as in the United States, the main emphasis tends to fall on basic skill testing. One complicating factor, of course, is that, in some of the provinces, French and English co-exist as first and as second languages, but it cannot be said that equal resources are devoted to their teaching, nor equal sophistication to their assessment. Most provincial language assessment programmes make use of a veritable rag-bag of tests, culled from the USA, the UK, France and Belgium, many of them of extremely dubious suitability for the native Canadian student population. Even those language tests which have been standardised locally tend to be very deficient from the psychometric standpoint, usually cast in a traditional multiple-choice format, and frequently almost Byzantine in the complexity of their items. Recently, there has been a courageous move in Ontario at least to supplement test data with the holistic assessment of students' expressive writing — a move greeted with considerable enthusiasm by the language teachers of the province. In Alberta, too, moves are now afoot to investigate the feasibility of assessing students' spoken proficiency in English, but these developments represent the most forward-looking aspects of the Canadian language assessment scene. In general, language assessment in Canada has tended to rely heavily on foreign expertise and it is only in the very recent past that efforts have been made to build up home-grown Canadian expertise in the field of psychometrics.

In both Canada and the USA, it is commonplace for educational authorities to issue teaching 'guidelines' which become the accepted norm for the province or state and which have a very influential effect indeed on curriculum development. In contrast to the state of opinion in this country, there is in North America a strong desire amongst teachers for a 'core curriculum' to be defined and elaborated by state or provincial education authorities. The official guidelines are regarded as a positive step in this direction/ They vary in the level of detail at which they are formulated but, on the whole, tend to err on the side of the comprehensive. In Ontario, Canada, for example, Ministry of Education guidelines are laid down for each of the main areas of the curriculum and are periodically revised. In the current guidelines (Ontario Ministry of Education, 1975) for the primary and junior levels of schooling, for instance, it is expected that, on completion of the English language programme, each child will have been given 'the opportunity to acquire competence' in certain carefully-defined areas of skill. Thus, in the case of listening skills, it is expected that, within the overall objective 'Listen with sensitivity and discrimination', the child should be able to:

locate, interpret, compare, classify, and discuss a variety of sounds;

recognise variations in intonation, volume, stress, pitch, and in the whole melody of speech;

recognise the qualities and textures of sound;

recognise a variety of language patterns, rhymes, sounds, and rhythms and make comparisons and find relationships;

differentiate sounds within words (phonics);

appreciate poetry and prose that is read aloud by others; and explore and interpret the human experience, feelings, and values expressed therein;

appreciate models of good speech and of the effective use of sound and music;

acquire an understanding of oral directions, messages, and reports.

Similarly, with regard to spoken skills, within the overall objective 'Articulate his or her own ideas, thoughts, and feelings with confidence and lucidity', the child is expected to be able to:

use speech to establish and maintain groups in which learning is likely to occur;

form ideas through impromptu talk, using incomplete and tentative structures if necessary:

master a vocabulary that enables him or her to name, describe, reason, explain, and use qualitative words as he or she plays, observes, manipulates, creates, and experiments with stimulating materials;

discuss topics and issues that are personally significant;

participate in dramatic play, puppetry, choral speech, and oral reading.

The three main objectives given for the acquisition of reading at the primary level are: 'Learn to read using the initial skills and processes that he or she finds most effective'; 'Appreciate the significance and function of reading in his or her own life'; and 'Read independently with enjoyment and with a fluency appropriate to his or her stage of development'. Each of these main objectives is then elaborated in detail.

The teaching of writing skills has only one main objective at the primary level, namely, to allow the child to 'express experiences, thoughts, and feelings in writing with clarity and sensitivity'. This is elaborated in detail as follows:

master a vocabulary of words, phrases, and expressions through which personal feelings, sensations and observations can be adequately expressed;

experiment with words, word patterns, and idioms;

develop a sense of sequence and logic that enables individual progress from isolated phrases or sentences to the coherence of a paragraph;

demonstrate an appreciation of style by incorporating in his or her own writing effective words or phrases selected from those encountered in reading and listening;

demonstrate a knowledge of the patterns of spelling and rules of punctuation required for clarity;

demonstrate a knowledge of common grammatical forms;

write legibly in a manner appropriate to his or her stage of development;

use writing for creative expression (eg stories and verses);

use writing for practical purposes (eg sequential instructions for specific operations or short letters requesting permission or information);

assess his or her own writing in appropriate ways;

appreciate that writing can be used to inform, to explain, to describe, to narrate, and to give voice to imagination and fantasy.

The Ontario Ministry of Education guidelines go on to lay down similarly-detailed objectives for older children and for other areas of the curriculum. They are only one example of their kind, but they are not untypical. Guidelines such as these are welcomed by the teaching profession and exert a profound effect on curriculum development and on the assessment of student performance. In an increasing number of instances, the careful definition of teaching objectives has gone hand-in-hand with the construction of banks of related test items, housed centrally but made available to schools throughout the state or province. This development seems to represent a growing tendency throughout North America, generally as the result of a creative, collaborative effort between practising teachers and experts in the field of educational measurement.

This is an area in which, in this country, we appear to fall far short of what is technically possible. In my experience, when language teachers and psychometricians meet on this side of the Atlantic, the attitude of the former tends to be epitomised in the somewhat paranoid: 'No-one is going to dictate to us what we can or cannot test'. This seems to me a narrow and mistaken view of the exciting possibilities that recent developments in assessment techniques have opened up for the linguist: for example, I have yet to meet a linguist in this country (apart from those working for the NFER, that is) who has any awareness at all of the scope offered to him or her by the potential richness of recently-developed item-banking techniques. This is not true on the other side of the Atlantic. In North America, the dialogue between language teachers and psychometricians seems far more constructive, productive and forward-looking than any of which I am aware in this country. And yet, we are well ahead of our American cousins in many areas of language assessment. I leave the gentle reader to draw the moral.

References

National Assessment of Educational Progress. *Reading: selected exercises.* Report 02-R-20. NAEP, Denver, Colorado, 1972.

Mead, N A. *Issues related to a national assessment of speaking and listening skills.* Paper presented at the Speech Communication Annual Convention, Washington, DC, December 1977.

Ontario Ministry of Education. *The formative years.* Circular P1J1. Ministry of Education, Toronto, 1975.

Appendix

NAEP list of assessment objectives

Informing/Speaking
1. Be able to choose an appropriate topic for an informative talk.
2. Be able to introduce a topic in an informative talk.
3. Be able to conclude effectively an informative talk.
4. Be able to organise an informative talk.
5. Be able to elaborate a point.
6. Be able to ask questions.
7. Be able to give directions.
8. Be able to describe objects, people, places and activities.

Informing/Listening
9. Be able to listen actively to and analyse an informative speech.
10. Be able to listen actively to an everyday informative message.

Controlling/Speaking
1. Be able to use persuasive arguments.
2. Be able to support a position with appropriate arguments.
3. Be able to support arguments with appropriate evidence.
4. Be able to analyse an audience.
5. Be able to distinguish facts from opinions.
6. Be able to identify logical arguments from illogical arguments.

Controlling/Listening
7. Be able to listen actively to and analyse a persuasive speech.
8. Be able to listen actively to an everyday persuasive message.

Sharing Feelings/Expressing
1. Be able to recognise if the situation is appropriate for sharing feelings.
2. Be able to assert feelings in difficult communication situations.

Sharing Feelings/Recognising
3. Be able to recognise non-verbal expression of typical feelings.
4. Be able to recognise incongruence between verbal and non-verbal expressions of typical feelings.

Ritualising
1. Be able to lead a group discussion.
2. Be able to identify ritual communications from other types of communication.
3. Be able to perform typical communication rituals.

Communicating Attitudes
1. Be willing to communicate with others.
2. Have a positive concept of self as a communicator.
3. Be willing to share feelings.
4. Be comfortable communicating in difficult communication situations (in front of large audiences, in groups, with authority figures or strangers).
5. Be comfortable when involved in persuasive communication.
6. Be comfortable when involved in communication rituals.
7. Be tolerant of different dialects and ways of communicating.

Reproduced from Mead, N A (1977) op cit

7. The education and training of teachers

A. Spicer
W.H. Mittins and
C.E. Dawson

(The following chapter consists of two main parts: the first by W.H. Mittins on teachers of English, the second by A. Spicer and C.E. Dawson on teachers of foreign languages. The introduction is by A. Spicer. Dr Mittins' part was originally prepared for a seminar of the British Association for Applied Linguistics and permission to incorporate it here is gratefully acknowledged)

Introduction

The present situation in the field of teacher education and training can be held up as a splendid example of the benefits of academic freedom where variety and experimentation can flourish in quasi-autonomous institutions unhampered by central direction. Alternatively it can be pilloried as a prime example of the unacceptable face of free (academic) enterprise where anything goes and which is characterised chiefly by the wide range in the quality of its output (probationary teachers) whose standards vary from the highest professional to the barely competent. A situation in which the relevant question to put to an applicant for a first teaching post is not 'what educational and professional training qualifications do you possess?' but rather 'where did you obtain them?'

There are few I think who would claim that all was well and although the opposite view that, in the current cant phrase, we are in a disaster situation is too extreme, even the middle of the road position must give us cause for concern and indicates the need for some action to be taken to raise standards. Unfortunately, however, for any would-be reformers, there is a noticeable absence of any consensus in the profession on a number of major issues, something which no doubt is one reason for the equally noticeable lack of forward planning and a reluctance to take decisions based on any other criteria than financial ones. This division of opinion among teachers and others concerned with language teaching obviously must affect any proposals for improving teacher education and training. For example, there is still no general agreement regarding:

(i) the role and functions of English as a curriculum subject;
(ii) the status of mother tongues other than English, Welsh and Gaelic[1] in the educational system (and of non-standard varieties of English);
(iii) which foreign languages for whom, when, for how long and for what purpose.

---

[1] Some uncertainties remain even about Welsh and Gaelic and indeed about English itself in certain areas in Wales and Scotland.

Again there is very considerable disagreement as to whether the overt and systematic teaching of English as the mother tongue is necessary or desirable. Similarly there is little agreement as to whether the teaching of foreign or second languages should be primarily based on a L1 (pre-school) acquisition model, a L1 (post-infancy) development model, a L2 acquisition-by-exposure model, or a more academic and/or cognitive FL learning model — or of course, on some judicious combination of models.

Thus it would be premature for the authors of this paper to come to firm or detailed conclusions regarding the form and content of the education and training that language teachers will need in the 1980s in a Britain which has become more multilingual, multicultural (and outward looking?) than most of us (including Robbins, James, Bullock *et al.*) seem to have fully appreciated.

However, when we take into account that there is no massively entrenched general feeling of satisfaction with the present provisions for teacher training; that on the contrary there is a growing feeling of crisis (amounting almost to panic in some quarters), and that we are now in the midst of yet another reorganisation of our training institutions, we are probably right to conclude the time is ripe to map out at least the general direction in which we want to travel and to prepare a selection of available alternative routes.

We are therefore offering this discussion paper as a contribution to the debate. Our paper has as its topic some of the possible implications for the education and training of future teachers of languages which, it seems to us, derive from the current situation with all its confusion and deficiencies and, more positively, which stem from the basic theme of language and languages in education.

Part 1: How professional are teachers of English

Criteria of professionalism

There is of course no straight answer to this question. It all depends . . . It all depends on:

(a) which teachers of English we have in mind;

(b) what we take 'professional' to mean;

(c) to what extent we are concerned with the professionalism of English-teachers as teachers in general;

(d) to what extent we are concerned with the professionalism of the specialist teachers of English within (a) above.

The answer to (a) must be arbitrary. I cannot in one paper, even if I were competent, deal with all teachers of English in all kinds of teaching institution. Let me therefore exclude the specialists in further and higher education, where they have comparatively specific and limited briefs. Let me also exclude primary school teachers, because they are non-specialists teaching many other things as well as English. This leaves me with the greatest category of the more or less specialist teachers of English, those who work in secondary schools.

The answer to (b) is less easy. There have been many attempts to identify the characteristics of a profession. Among these is a list provided by the American National Association of Education (1948). This list, with some slight modification, should serve my purpose as well as any. It proposes that a profession:

(1) involves activities which are essentially intellectual;
(2) commands a body of specialised knowledge;
(3) requires extended professional (as contrasted with solely general) preparation;
(4) demands continuous in-service growth;
(5) affords a life career and permanent membership;
(6) sets up its own standards;
(7) has a strong, closely knit, professional organisation;
(8) exalts service above personal gain.

I have changed the NEA's order of the last two items, so that I may the more easily drop (8), thereby enabling me to argue with greater conviction that established professions like medicine and law, with which teaching commonly aspires to be equated, measure up well to the total requirements. (This is not to suggest that a sense of public service is not conspicuous among many doctors, lawyers, and indeed teachers. But since 1948, when the NEA list was first published, there has been such an approximation in emphasis and outlook between professions and trades unions as to make this criterion less applicable.) The only other amendment to the list that I would favour would be to add a criterion of continuous self-criticism. But perhaps it can be assumed that the essential intellectual activities in (1) include it and that the in-service growth in (4) would be impossible without it.

This leaves my questions (c) and (d). The distinctions between them, between the general professionalism of all secondary-school teachers and the specific profession-alism of subject-specialists would be more manageable with almost any other subject than English, for reasons to be mentioned later. Let me postpone consideration of (d) until I have considered how well, compared with medicine and law, teaching satisfies the listed criteria. It is convenient to take them in reverse order, from the more general and organisational to the more specific and academic. My answers to the seven questions must inevitably be generalisations and therefore rough — but I hope not rude in anything but the sense in which rude also means 'more or less'.

The satisfaction of criterion (7) cannot be claimed with any conviction; not only is there no single teachers' organisation, but the largest of the existing handful are hardly strong or closely-knit in the way the medical and legal equivalents are. Reservations increase over criterion (6). Teachers are only partially responsible for standards in their work. Examinations, demands of parents, of employers, of further and higher education, views of advisers and inspectors, control by Local Education Authorities, and most recently governmental pressure through the Great Debate of 1977/8 and the Assessment of Performance Unit — all these, for good or ill, have contributed, do contribute or will contribute to the determination of standards. There is in-service growth (4) in teaching, but only on a scale that falls far short of aspirations and stated intentions — and indeed of needs. Nor can the answer to (3) be a whole-hearted yes. Specific training for teaching is only part of 'concurrent'

Certificate and BEd courses in colleges of education, where such programmes, lasting over three or four years, are also largely concerned with academic studies; under 'consecutive' arrangements, graduates are trained in PGCE courses for one brief academic year. It is difficult to describe either amount of preparation as 'extended'. But the three-year first degree course and the academic studies component of college courses can reasonably be considered to satisfy requirement (2). (It is not necessary here to make the further distinction between the academic study of teaching subjects and that of aspects of educational theory and practice, though such a distinction would make it possible to argue that college courses satisfy (2) much more substantially than do PGCE courses.) Given a reasonably broad definition of 'essentially intellectual' activities under (1), teachers *qua* teachers could be allowed to rate well.

On my additional criterion of self-criticism, teaching compares less favourably with the accepted 'learned' professions. It is true that team-teaching procedures and an increase in departmental and staff meetings have probably brought an increased willingness in many teachers openly to discuss professional problems and even critically to watch each other at work. Nevertheless, the traditional concept of the specialist classroom private to the specialist teacher using it persists.

Teachers are notoriously reluctant to make objective criticisms of the curriculum as a whole and to examine educational issues transcending their particular subject-interests.

Daniel Fader blames 'the myths, customarily paired for strength, of the teacher as individualist and the classroom as castle' for doing 'more harm to the profession of teaching than any other combination of ideas or events'. Consequently:

> Unlike conventions of other professions I have attended, where the wolves eat the rabbits at one bite, the teaching profession convenes only rabbits and nobody eats anybody. In short, public criticism of one teacher by another is as little encountered in the so-called profession at conventions as it is in the so-called profession in schools. It is exactly this absence of interior criticism that causes the profession to remain so-called. (Fader, 1966)

English language responsibilities

The reason why in the area of English it is difficult clearly to separate general from specialist functions in the way they can be separated in other subject areas is the circumstance that the native language is not only the prime concern of the English specialist but also, because it is the medium through which the whole curriculum is taught and learned, the general concern of all teachers. This area of concern spans both (c) and (d) in my initial short set of questions. It is the area of language across the curriculum. It is an area rather cautiously explored in the Bullock Report (1975). This report espoused the cause of a general responsibility among teachers for the language development and competence of students, and there is some evidence that the movement towards school language policies is spreading, albeit slowly. But the question of assigning responsibility for it is a delicate one. The Bullock Committee recognised the need to enlist the support and influence of the school Head, but it tentatively offered a number of different suggestions about where leadership in initiating policy-making and implementation should be located. One possibility is for the operation to be controlled by a senior member of staff, perhaps one already designated director of studies or curriculum coordinator. Instead, or perhaps as well, a committee might be set up for the job. The Report (12.12) hesitates to assign direction to the English department, partly because that department is probably hard-pressed enough already, partly because 'in some schools such an arrangement might make it harder for the concept to win acceptance among the staff'. Nevertheless, 'it would be important to establish a proper working relationship with the head of English department, whose own contribution must clearly be a considerable one'. Certainly, any committee would include the head of English, perhaps with heads of other departments and the Head teacher.

If we were not so used to the variegated, amorphous character of the subject called 'English' and to the deep and long-standing differences among teachers of English about the content and focus of their subject, we should surely be astonished that the Bullock Committee found it necessary or diplomatic to tread so warily. To the uninitiated it might seem automatic to give major responsibility for a major native language project to teachers of native language. Could it be that the Bullock Committee seriously doubted whether English specialists could speak with the necessary authority in language matters?

It would not be surprising if this were so, for reasons not far to seek. Most English specialists, like most teachers, have probably spent little time in the study of the vernacular. Some of the older ones will have been taught some English grammar (probably on discredited parts-of-speech and clause analysis lines); they may also have explained alleged 'errors' in concocted sentences and worked other language exercises in order to get a School Certificate (later 'O' level) pass at age sixteen. For most, that would be the end of their linguistic studies. From a small minority of the rest the Associated Examining Board's 'A' level English paper might have demanded some theoretical language work. But the great majority of potential teachers, including younger ones and potential specialist teachers of English (and including the comparative few who may have taken a 'Use of English' examination for university entrance), will have confined their school 'English' operations to using the language rather than studying it. A similar emphasis will have prevailed during teacher training, though a few colleges of education and a growing number of universities include language study in their certificate and degree programmes. In these circumstances, hesitation to assign a major language job primarily to those teachers who *prima facie* should have the expertise and authority to undertake it is very understandable. It is also very regrettable. The fault lies, of course, not in the specialist teachers themselves, but in the system through which they have proceeded to their posts. Inevitably they are open to the charge of being professionally ill-equipped, but it is their education and preparation as teachers that have inadequately equipped them.

A defence against this harsh accusation could be based on the very concession made in the Bullock Report — that the English department is hard-pressed enough without undertaking a large new commitment. Consideration of the 'hard pressure' referred to takes us right into the area — my (d) — of specialist English-teaching. In this area, English in the pre-sixth form classes of secondary schools comprises mainly:

(a) the use of language, spoken and written, in productive composition, talk and discussion;

(b) reading and comprehension at various levels and in various kinds;

(c) the study of literature, including drama (or at least dramatic texts).

This list is doubtless incomplete, but it is formidable enough without the additions that would make it comprehensive.

In addition to having 'knowledge-that' in all these special areas, English-teachers are required to have 'know-how'. Just as teachers of art and craft subjects ought to be reasonably good artists and craftsmen, so the Englisher ought to have real command of the spoken and written English language.

The content of 'English'

This range of required expertise makes one very sympathetic to the work-load argument. But it leaves open to question the English-teacher's expertise in teaching language, in the sense of enabling and helping his students to achieve a reasonable command of the vernacular. The question is complicated. One aspect of it is the age-old dispute between those who see language merely as the 'handmaiden' of literature and those who contrariwise see literature as only one, albeit an important, rich and complex one, of the many 'registers' of language. To extremist advocates of the centrality of literature, language competence (as well as more valuable humanistic qualities) comes mainly from exposure to and contact with great works of literary art. To extremist promulgators of the centrality of language, literature provides (in addition to those same humanistic values, and no less important than them) material for linguistic study and analysis. Most specialist teachers of English occupy inter-mediate positions between these extremes; some believe that 'English' subsumes both in a unitary subject. It is not necessary for me here to explore further this crudely delineated battlefield. The relevant point is that English specialists have a professional responsibility to explore it. Their job is, not to take up a predetermined stance on one side or the other, but to understand the issues involved and come to a balanced, reasonable accommodation. Such understanding involves awareness and appreciation of both sides. Too often, the English teacher's professionalism is more obvious in literature than in language matters.

Related to this vexed problem of the literature/language relationship is the no less difficult distinction between the study of language and the use of it. A considerable amount of empirical research has seemed to show fairly conclusively that the study of grammar (by any definition a major component of language) brings no improvement, and may even be conducive to deterioration, in language performance. Reservations about the character of the grammar studies may cast doubts on the validity of the alleged proof. It was usually parts-of-speech grammar of a dubious kind, and teaching suspect grammar does not discredit the possible usefulness of a better grammar. But reservations about the timing of the teaching — was it taught prematurely? — could apply to any kind of grammar, or indeed to other aspects of language study. It is certainly possible that the syntax of English is so complex that learners capable of understanding it don't much need its help in using language, whereas conversely learners incompetent in using language may not benefit from studying it. Again, it is

94

not for me to argue one way or the other. But, in order to solve the problem in a professional way, teachers of English need to understand fully the factors involved. There is reason to believe that many English specialists do not know enough about language properly to appreciate the relevant issues.

A third problem arises in the 'know-how' area. There is a nice, tentative near-ambiguity in the Bullock Report's comment (23.23) on the command of English of teacher-trainees: 'In our view the teacher's competence in all aspects of language should be beyond question'. Not only is 'all aspects of language' susceptible of elastic interpretation, but 'should be beyond question' might be taken either optimistically as a largely favourable endorsement of an existing state of affairs or pessimistically as a tactful hint that some teachers' competence in language is distinctly questionable. The fact that the sentence immediately follows references to complaints by heads of schools about standards of written English among college of education students and some young teachers sadly supports the pessimistic view. It echoes remarks made at the very beginning of the Report, where the dissatisfactions of employers, of staff in institutions of further and higher education, and of an examiner of college of education students are added to those of heads of schools (1.2, 1.3). (We who work in universities would not care to claim exemption from these criticisms for all our students, postgraduate and higher degree as well as undergraduate, or indeed for all our colleagues.) This is not intended to reinforce the jeremiads of those who claim to see a woeful decline in recent years in standards of language use. The comparisons properly to be made are not against the past. Measurement should be 'against the demands of a professional function' (Bullock Report, i.3). In an age when verbal communication is quantitatively more widespread and qualitatively more demanding, it is not at all surprising that levels of verbal performance often fall short of what is necessary and desirable. It is none the less the teaching profession's duty to recognise this shortfall and to take steps to eliminate it. And within the teaching body teachers of English have the major responsibility in working for improvement. As before, the prime and immediate need is not for teachers to devise quick solutions so much as for them to understand the issues involved and evaluate the various measures and policies proposed.

Through models to rationale

These three problematic areas, along with others not specifically mentioned, add up to a considerable challenge to teachers of English, particularly specialists, to resolve long-standing disagreements about the nature and rationale of their subject. A fair number — perhaps disproportionately frequent among the one-third of secondary school teachers of English who 'have no discernible qualification for the role' (Bullock Report, 15.14) — like a fair number of other teachers, probably do not concern themselves overmuch with thinking out rationales. They teach English in the way expected of them by their schools, or in the way they were themselves taught as pupils, or in the way the available text-books seem to require, or in the way personal predilection or prejudice dictates. Their choice among the roles offered by Andrew Wilkinson (1963) — as Grendel's mother ('guardian of the word-hoard'), as sergeant-major (Keep Fit Exercises in English), as Sigmund Freud (exercise book = case book), as group-therapist (play out your problems), as actor-manager (classroom as theatre), as printer's reader (proof-corrector), or whatever else — is made more or less unreflectingly. Unfortunately, similar differences prevail among those teachers of English, including presumably all heads of English departments, who do hold thought-out convictions on the nature and purpose of English-teaching.

The famous Anglo-American Dartmouth Seminar in 1966 apparently highlighted these differences. In *Growth through English* (1967), based on the Dartmouth discussions, John Dixon identifies three 'models or images of English that have been widely accepted in schools on both sides of the Atlantic' (p.1).

In chronological order, these models focused on language skills, then on the cultural heritage, then on personal growth. In turn they were primarily concerned with initial literacy, great literature, and the creative use of language; in other and more grandiose words, with communication, culture, and individual development. To a considerable extent, history supports Dixon's contention that each 'model' replaced its predecessor. What is more disputable, and more important, is the extent to which each, in doing so, subsumed —or discarded — its predecessor(s). Dixon argues that the prime objective of the first model, initial literacy, was achieved in the 'almost universal literacy in our countries' (p.2), leaving a vacuum to be filled by the 'cultural heritage' approach. This in turn deteriorated into 'marginal annotations and essay notes' on approved works of literature (p.3) and was superseded by the 'personal growth' preoccupation with the learner's exploration of experience with language. The existence today of a large adult illiteracy problem makes the claim to have achieved widespread universal literacy ring somewhat hollow, even on the most generous interpretation of 'literacy'. It is only fair to note, however, that Dixon recognises the failure of the 'cultural heritage' model, when it took over, 'to reinterpret the concept of ''skills''' (p.4). He does not seem similarly to recognise the failure of his third — 'personal growth' — model to reinterpret the roles both of the skills and of literature study.

Other models, or at least movements or trends, have emerged in recent years. Some teachers of English have so emphasised the social dimension of their subject that it has tended to approximate to 'social studies' (or what David Riesman called 'social slops'), a subject which has been accused of being even less clearly defined than English. In a few schools, I understand, the English department has actually been absorbed by the Social Studies department. Arguably, a rather less dreadful fate is to be swallowed up by Humanities. Running counter to all these movements is the trend sponsored by the Great Debate, with its crude and ill-defined stress on the 'basics' of literacy. It seems only too likely that the Assessment Unit of the DES will, whatever its long-term aims, soon add its weight, through selection of elements of language which are more readily measurable, to concentration on the conventions or 'decencies' of transactional prose. It cannot reasonably be denied that increased attention to the conventions of spelling, punctuation and sentence structure is long overdue, but such attention, however necessary, is not sufficient. These things need tackling in the context of continuous composition and as part of total language use, productive and receptive, spoken and written.

The one element common to all 'models' and movements in English — to the four skills of speaking, listening, writing and reading, to the study of literature and drama, to the 'utility' reading of newspapers and instructions on baked-beans tins, to expressive, transactional and poetic modes of writing — is the English language. Does this mean that all teachers of English, and certainly English specialists, should be conversant with those aspects of language study, of linguistics, that have relevance to the educational process? The obvious answer is yes. It is an answer given more readily by professional linguists than by teachers, many of whom have a deep-seated distrust of linguistics (partly, probably, because linguistics claims to be the scientific study of language, and science of any sort is still often seen as threatening to the literature-based English specialist). There has been an explosive increase in linguistic studies this century, especially in the United States, and in some ways this metaphorical explosion is as daunting as more literal ones. As one 'school' of linguists succeeds another in rapid succession, as traditional grammar yields to structural, which is swallowed up in transformational-generative, which is (perhaps) overtaken by stratificational and case grammars, the English teacher is right to be wary.

It is not, of course, the job of linguisticians to tell English teachers what to teach or indeed what they should know about their subject. Nevertheless, it would be a bold English specialist (and there are quite a few such) who could deny any validity at all to the barrage of criticisms of English-teaching that has come over the years from linguistic quarters. In a speech to the Linguistic Society of America as long ago as 1924, Bloomfield expressed the view that:

> Our schools are conducted by persons who, from professors of education down to teachers in the classrooms, know nothing of the results of linguistic science, not even the relation of writing to speech or of standard language to dialect. In short, they do not know what language is, and yet must teach it, and in consequence waste years of every child's life and reach a poor result. (1925)

This is a fierce charge. Both the degree of generalisation and the choice of exemplification (writing and speech, standard and dialect) surely make it less applicable to today's teachers. But it is by no means wholly unjust. A milder but also more positive and more specific expression of the same attitude came over thirty years later from another American, H.B. Allen:

> It may already be insisted upon that no prospective teacher of English should honestly consider himself prepared for his job unless he has some clear understanding of linguistic principles and some awareness of the implication of linguistics for his teaching of punctuation, grammar, vocabulary, spelling, composition, and literature. (1958)

These structures, aimed at American teachers of English, were and are without doubt equally applicable to their British counterparts. In fact, coming nearer to the here and now, we find our own J.L.M. Trim making very similar observations:

> It can almost certainly be said that the man in the street is better informed about nuclear physics, cosmology and genetics than about the language he uses and hears all day and every day . . . .
>
> A large part of the responsibility for this sad state of affairs must lie with the teaching of English in schools and even at university. English language at

'O' level is purely a matter of expressive and receptive skills, and at 'A' level does not exist. Teachers, for whom language is the primary professional tool, and who consequently stand to gain most from a conscious awareness of its nature and use, too rarely have any opportunity for the systematic study of language in their academic education and professional training. (1975)

The opportunities for systematic study of language could be increased by instituting an 'A' level English examination and by requiring all teachers to take a basic language course on the lines suggested in the Bullock Report (23.25). But such courses need to be designed and taught by people capable of extracting from the various branches of linguistics (including so-called educational linguistics) those elements most relevant to teaching and learning — relevant, that is, not as material to be directly taught, but as knowledge which contributes from a position '*behind* the classroom teacher, in the training that he receives for his job as a teacher, in the preparation of the syllabus according to which his teaching programme is organised, and in the preparation of the teaching materials of all kinds that he makes use of in class'. (Halliday, McIntosh and Strevens, 1964)

This is a tall order to make of busy people. Nevertheless, if the recommendations of the Bullock Report are to be taken seriously — and all but a comparative few exclusively literature-minded specialists seem to accept these recommendations in general, if not in every detail — it is imperative that language policies be developed and implemented within schools. In this undertaking it is clearly the professional business primarily of English specialists to take the lead. If they fail, 'English' is likely to remain the predicament or even the 'disaster area' that it has been called.

Meanwhile, the answer to my initial question — How professional are teachers of English? — must be 'not very' or 'far too little'.

References to part 1

Allen, H.B. Foreword to *Readings in applied English Linguistics*. Appleton-Century-Crofts, 1958. p ix.

Bloomfield, L. 'Why a linguistic society.' *Language*, I, (1925). p 5.

Committee of Inquiry into Reading and the Use of English. *A language for life*. HMSO, 1975. (The Bullock Report.)

Dixon, J. *Growth through English*. Oxford University Press for the National Association for the Teaching of English, 1967.

Fader, D.N. *Hooked on books*. Pergamon Press, 1966. p 26.

Halliday, M.A.K., McIntosh, A., and Strevens, P. *The linguistic sciences and language teaching*. Longmans, 1964, p 187.

National Education Association. 'The yardstick of a profession.' Division of Field Service, 1948. Quoted in *The professional problems of teachers* by T.M. Stinnett. Macmillan, 1968.

Trim, J.L.M. Review of books on linguistics in *Times Higher Education Supplement*, 28 March 1971.

Wilkinson, Andrew. 'Roles and analogies in teaching English.' *Educational Review*, 16, 1, 1963, pp 55–62.

Part 2: The education and training of teachers of modern foreign languages: principles and problems

1. Why the professional training of foreign language teachers should not be considered in isolation

Part 2 of this paper is concerned mainly with the education and training that future teachers of modern foreign languages in junior, middle and secondary schools in England receive — or perhaps more importantly, with the education and training they do not receive. Therefore in drawing attention to what we consider to be the main strengths and weaknesses of the preparation for a career in foreign language teaching that students are likely to be given in our universities, polytechnics, colleges and institutes of higher education we shall not focus exclusively on the initial foreign language methodology training provided by these institutions. Nor shall we lose sight of the fact that in England foreign language teaching at school takes place within a context where another language, usually English and usually (but certainly not always) the pupils' mother tongue is both the main language of instruction and a compulsory curriculum subject. For it is our contention that if we are to improve the quality of foreign language teaching in our schools we must take a wider view of what learning a language entails, a view which embraces all aspects of language study and use right across the curriculum, and which takes into account the varied but related linguistic demands made on both learners and teachers by this wide range of activities. Merely to review the content of the special method component that is offered exclusively to the intending foreign language teacher as part of his initial training would not be sufficient. We believe that this wider view of language learning and teaching in the school context will provide a useful basis for defining what should constitute a proper preparation for entry into the academic profession of foreign language teaching because:

(i) foreign language teachers like all teachers are educators first and subject specialists second;

(ii) with only the possible exception of some very specialised courses, foreign language teachers are inescapably teachers of more than language;

(iii) *all* teachers are willy-nilly teachers of language;

(iv) many of the methodological problems confronting the foreign language teacher also confront the teacher of English as the mother tongue (and indeed confront the teaching profession as a whole), eg problems of individualisation of teaching, of mixed ability classes, of the specification and differentiation of objectives, of teacher-learner interaction, of the identification, explanation and treatment of learners' errors, of motivation, of relating what is taught in a particular class to the rest of the curriculum and to the 'real world' outside the school, etc, etc;

(v) teachers of modern foreign languages, of English as a foreign or second language and of English as the mother tongue have something to learn from each others' successes and failures at all levels (aims, approaches, methods, techniques and assessment procedures);

99

(vi) cooperation between teachers of all subjects in matters of language use offers possibilities of mutually supportive activities aimed at improving the quality of communication (fluency, appropriateness, sensitivity and accuracy) in all aspects of school life;

(vii) the initial professional training of teachers cannot sensibly be looked at in isolation from the previous or concurrent academic education they have received (or are receiving) nor from the subsequent in-service training they will (or should) receive;

(viii) the best chance we have to raise the standards of language teaching is to improve the status of the school teaching profession as a whole, to make it a more 'professional' profession (cf part 1 of this paper).

2. Why it is appropriate at this time to review yet again the education and training of language teachers

It is an appropriate development of applied linguistics. At various periods in the recent history of the discipline the spotlight has in turn fallen on methods, on materials and aids, on analyses of the target and native languages, on testing, and more recently still (and very properly) on the learner, his interlanguage, his learning strategies, his motivations, his inhibitions and his interactions with his teachers and fellow learners as well as on the design of syllabuses suited to his particular needs and abilities. During this time we have acquired at least the beginnings of wisdom (as well as a great deal of knowledge) and we no longer expect to discover the universal method which will solve all problems. We no longer underestimate the learners' contribution to the learning processes, but it is to be hoped that this does not mean we shall fall into the trap of undervaluing the role of the teacher by directing most of our attention to just one of the many variables in the language learning/teaching situation. Thus, while we are proposing that the time is ripe to look carefully again at the role of the teacher, we are not suggesting that we should repeat the mistakes of the past and concentrate exclusively on one single factor. Somehow we must keep all the different variables in mind and pay proper attention to each of them. Indeed we neglect the teacher factor at our peril and if we fail to give him the kind of education, training and support his key position demands the whole edifice crumbles. We believe that there is some evidence of neglect and that consequently we may already be seeing the beginnings of potentially serious disintegration.

The time is now ripe since once again the teaching both of foreign languages and the mother tongue is under attack from politicians of all parties, from parents, education authorities, inspectors, students and perhaps most significantly from some of the teachers themselves. Of course these attacks take very different forms and while both mother tongue and foreign language teaching are alleged by some critics to be inefficient, others go further and claim that the teaching of foreign languages at school is unnecessary and undesirable. When we say that language teaching is under attack from some language teachers we are not so much thinking of those who challenge currently popular approaches and methods, but rather of those who doubt whether it is appropriate to teach the native language *qua* language at all and of those who doubt whether it is possible to teach a foreign language to any but the most academically gifted pupils. This is not the occasion to go into the rights and wrongs of such attacks and it is sufficient for our present purposes to take note of what is at the very least evidence of a growing crisis of confidence both within and outside the profession.

There may also be at this time a crisis of numbers (the evidence one way or the other is not clear) but what is certain is that while more pupils than ever before are starting a foreign language at school, too many are 'voting with their feet' and opting out at the earliest opportunity — a state of affairs which must surely, to some extent at least, suggest that there are deficiencies in the teaching.

Sadly it is also appropriate to look again at teacher training at this time because of the decimation of the colleges of education and of yet another reorganisation of these very hard-done-by institutions. Nevertheless the present situation with the reduction in the number of teachers the country is prepared to afford, does give us the opportunity to raise standards both at entry and at the time of final qualification.

We are not, of course, claiming that all the ills of language teaching are due to the failings of the teachers — nor shall we leap aboard the 'blame-the-teacher' bandwagon which appears to be gathering momentum. Nor again do we wish to apportion blame elsewhere. We are all to blame — or rather we are all responsible in one way or another for what has happened. And when we say all we mean all: politicians, DES, the inspectorate, the LEAs, the teacher trainers, the universities — everyone involved in deciding what education and training our future language teachers shall receive. Not so much perhaps because of sins of commission but rather of omission, of apathy, of neglect. We often say let us cherish our pupils: let us also remind ourselves that we should cherish our teachers. And cherishing involves the judicious use both of rewards and the withholding of rewards as well as the provision of adequate training and in-service support.

3. Principles

The basic skills and knowledge that it is reasonable to expect a teacher of a foreign language to possess can be summarised briefly (and we would think uncontroversially) as follows:

   (i) a fluent and accurate command of the spoken and written language he is teaching;
  (ii) knowledge of the rules governing grammaticality and appropriateness in the foreign language, ie how that language functions;
 (iii) experience of and sensitivity towards appropriate aspects of the civilisation and way of life of the peoples whose language it is;
 (iv) a conscious awareness of the significant differences between the foreign language and the native language and between the foreign and native cultures;
  (v) knowledge of the language learning processes in general and, in particular, of the learning strategies and problems of the pupils he is teaching;
 (vi) knowledge and experience of language teaching methods and materials and of assessment procedures appropriate to the learners and to the teaching situations he is concerned with.

Details of what should be included under each of these headings would, of course, be more controversial, but again this is not the occasion for a detailed discussion of such matters. What we hope would be both uncontroversial and appropriate at this point is a general statement of principle, namely that to ensure that our foreign language teachers possess the skills and knowledge outlined above we must see that they receive a specialised education and a professional training that is comparable both in extent and quality to that given in other professions (eg law, medicine, psychology, etc).

It would be more difficult to make a similar brief summary of what we should expect of the teacher of the native language since there appears to be far less general agreement concerning the aims of mother tongue teaching at school. This important matter is the subject of part 1 of this paper, but as we have indicated in sections 1 and 2 above, we would wish to underline that some areas of education and training ought to be common to both L1 and FL teachers and that the same standards of professionalism should apply in both cases.

To be really comparable with the education and training demanded of and provided for the lawyer, the doctor, the professional psychologist, etc we will need to ensure that all entrants to our profession have received:

(a) An adequate education in the relevant disciplines to the level of the Bachelor's degree or its equivalent (BA, BEd or BSc schemes of study which include substantial components in relevant areas of linguistics, literature (or other civilisation studies) and education (or another cognate discipline) See 5 *A, B & C below*);

(b) an adequate training in the relevant language skills to a level to be specified;

(c) an adequate period of 'structured experience' of living and working in the foreign country (either as part of their specialist education or their professional training);

(d) an adequate professional training including:

(i) language learning and language teaching theories, ie relevant aspects of the psychology and sociology of language and of applied linguistics (eg language teaching methodology, syllabus and materials design and evaluation, error analysis and explanation, testing, etc);

(ii) teaching practice in the foreign language in relevant teaching situations;

(iii) supervision and guidance during teaching practice from experienced practitioners who themselves are teaching, or who have had recent experience of teaching, in those situations;

(iv) assessment of practical performance by specialists in their own field of foreign language teaching and according to a defined system of assessment;

(v) continued in-service support and training after the initial phase together with further assessment of progress and achievement.

Uncontroversial and indeed obvious as all this is, what guarantees does the present system give us that these necessary conditions are always met?

4. The training of foreign language teachers — the present situation

Any attempt to present a brief general account of the initial training of modern language teachers in the UK will inevitably fail to reflect adequately the considerable variations to be found in what might at first glance seem to be a relatively restricted field of enquiry. What follows is based principally upon information provided by about half the institutions approached in 1977/8 (some 100 in all) on behalf of the NCLE. Hence account is taken of work going on in university departments of education preparing for the PGCE, and in the colleges (mostly now 'of higher education') where some teacher's certificate work remains, but BEd is rapidly becoming the rule. the latter however may be a three or four year course, the first two years of which will in certain cases consist of a Dip HE course not specifically designed for the training of teachers. Again, in the case of modular courses, the teacher-training pathway may overlap with eg general BA work and be somewhat difficult to identify. Add to this the major difference between the consecutive and the concurrent course, recall also the very interesting variations to be found 'north of the Border', note, finally, that student-teachers may be aiming at primary, middle school or secondary careers — and it becomes clear that any kind of generalisation becomes perilous indeed, at best impressionistic, and at worst grossly oversimplified.

First it should be observed that most courses have in view 'the modern-language teacher', knowing that in practice French will be markedly dominant, and making reduced, often *ad hoc*, provision for the methodology of teaching other languages. Whether aims are explicitly stated or implicit in the description of the general approach, content and methods of working, it is safe to say that initial-training courses place much emphasis on preparing students for the oral approach to modern language teaching. There invariably seems to be some attention to 'principles' (with, in some cases, an introduction to general linguistic theory) but more often than not the course proceeds rapidly to a consideration of the four major skills. Somewhere — often in the general professional area — time is almost always given to a post-Bullock element entitled, for example, 'Language and education' or 'Language in school'. This is frequently compulsory for all students and may be staffed by a team of tutors, in which modern linguists occasionally participate. The latter certainly appear to take note of such work and its connection with their own. Both psycholinguistic and sociolinguistic material will be included, and it is striking that, in the bibliographies, standard names tend to appear: Barnes, Britton, Chomsky, Wallwork, Wilkinson, Halliday, Stubbs, Trudgill . . .

The so-called four basic skills are usually considered from the dual standpoint of the pupil (ie how they are learned) and of the teacher (how best they may be taught). The latter involves systematic attention to classroom techniques, which seem to be universally stressed, and many courses involve contact with children prior to and in between the block practice or practices, by bringing pupils into the department or college, or taking students into the schools. There is the occasional case of a tutor who is at the same time a half-time teacher in a local school, or of tutors who put in a stint of classroom teaching from time to time; it is not uncommon for local teachers to be brought into supplement the work of tutors, and 'minority' languages are sometimes dealt with by this means.

Another standard feature is the attention given to analysis and discussion of commercially available material. This of course includes the study of audio-visual and audio-lingual courses, and major offerings such as 'Nuffield' — it also includes work on more traditional material however, and the department with a particular hobby-horse seems to be rare: given the sheer quantity of what is available, the eclectic approach seems to be the norm. Some programmes offer a methodical presentation of the whole range of classroom activities and exercises (eg question/answer technique, aural and written comprehension, guided composition, multiple-choice, the teaching of pronunciation, of grammar, of vocabulary, practice in phonetic work . . . the list can be considerable . . .).

Specific attention is normally given to planning the individual lesson, to problems of mixed-ability work, to the needs of the less able, to background studies. A mention of testing and examining is always to be found, and may include the levels of CSE, 'O' and 'A'. European studies and sixth form work usually find a place, as do — briefly — more marginal items such as the work of the Assistant, foreign correspondents and exchanges. The problem does seem to be, not what to include, but what may reasonably be left out.

As for the teaching methods adopted in colleges and departments, the traditional lecture is still to be found, but it is frequently noted that seminar groups, discussion, and when appropriate a workshop approach are preferred. The latter term is used when students are involved in working together on, for example, the production of supplementary materials (much time seems to be spent in this way) such as visuals, work-sheets, background materials or a learning kit. Micro-teaching sessions receive quite frequent mention, and in some places play a prominent part.

A wide range of equipment is normally presented to and handled by students, from the obvious tape-recorder to the projector, OHP, and language laboratory. For all these, there is usually practice in the provision of soft-ware.

It is interesting to note, also, that practice is given — in apparently a few places only — in the use of the foreign language, sometimes with the help of the Assistant. In one case reported upon, this amounted to a substantial proportion of the time available, and concerned a minor language. It is difficult to say how much time and effort is given to the teaching of languages other than French; one gets the impression that the attempt is often consciously made to encourage them, and indeed to keep them in being. On the whole, however, methodology of foreign language teaching seems to be a global concept. Mention should also be made of those places where experience of learning a previously unknown language formed part of the course, Welsh, Russian and Chinese being quoted.

Assessment of the modern language course is rarely if ever, it would appear, by means of formal examination, but rather on the basis of regular course assignments and practical exercises, plus perhaps one or more longer essays or projects. In addition students may be assessed on dossiers of teaching material compiled during the course, and on visual aids or kits which they have devised. A crucial element in the overall assessment is of course the teaching-practice, and some use is also made of the oral or viva. In connection with teaching-practice, a degree of divergence is noticeable, principally whether this consists of a single block or whether it is divided into two separate blocks in different schools. It appears to be a widespread custom to give students, even on the post-graduate year, experience of more than one school, and age-range.

In spite, therefore, of a large measure of agreement on the need for school and classroom orientated teacher education, there is considerable variation when it comes to the organisation and content of the courses. As between the BEd course of three or four years, and the alternative route of a first degree followed by a post-graduate year, there are obvious differences of rhythm, perhaps also of intensity, as well as those occasioned by the different patterns of school-practice experience which are a further consequence. Again, the university department may differ in the number of staff available to cover the several major aspects of the course, and colleges — often possessing a large education department — may offer a more elaborate programme and a greater time allocation to the professional, as opposed to the special-subject, side. A further and still controversial issue for the colleges, it should be recalled, is the question of the consecutive as opposed to the concurrent design for initial-training courses. As for a period of residence abroad, this seems to be specified only in a few cases, though it may be an unofficial requirement provided that sufficient applicants are forthcoming. A CNAA course is likely to be firm about this, but it is rarely the case that a period of study abroad is built into the programme in, for example, the BEd degree, during term time; whatever the shortcomings, vacation time and the 'Assistant year' seem often to be relied upon.

In conclusion, the comment has been made from more than one source, that the post-graduate year in particular imposes an enormous and perhaps unreasonable burden on students and tutors alike. In the attempt to prepare our students for their multifarious and to some extent unpredictable professional futures, we may (in the words of one tutor) be trying to offer 'practically a complete apprenticeship'. Some centrally agreed rationalisation of the links between initial training, the induction year, and later in-service work, seems highly desirable.

5. Problems
We now wish to refer briefly to some areas of the teachers' education and training where there may be ground for doubting whether adequate professional standards are always achieved.

A. The teacher's competence and performance in the foreign language
Although most universities, polytechnics and colleges now include an oral test as part of the final degree/certificate assessment, in most cases weakness in this area can be compensated for in other areas, eg literature, translation, etc. Also as the weighting given to these oral tests varies considerably from institution to institution it is often quite possible for a candidate to achieve a good overall result even if his oral performance is poor. Even when considerable attention is given to oral training the special classroom register of the language is often neglected and there are many teachers who cannot, for example, cope with the semi-technical vocabulary of audio and visual aids in the foreign language. Furthermore even the teaching practice assessment does not necessarily include a test of the candidate's ability to conduct

a lesson in the foreign language — indeed not all student teachers are guaranteed teaching practice in their foreign language (see 5D below).

Thus is it still possible in 1978 for someone to become a qualified teacher and teach a foreign language without ever having demonstrated that he is capable of sustaining a conversation in that language, let alone whether he is capable of conducting a lesson in it or that his pronunciation is acceptable as a model for his pupils. Many, possibly the majority, are fluent and accurate speakers of the foreign language, but a minority, possibly a sizeable minority, are not.

With regard to the ability of the new recruit to the profession to write the foreign language accurately and acceptably it may well be that in 1978 this is less of a problem than in the past and that the possession of a degree in a foreign language is usually a sufficient guarantee. However, again owing to the possibility of compensating for weakness in one area by excellence in another, it is still possible to become a teacher of a foreign language on the strength of a degree which has been awarded in spite of poor performance in the written language. And experience inclines us to believe that this is even more possible in the case of certificate courses at some colleges. One also has to remember that *all* degree schemes in foreign languages are acceptable as a basic qualification for entry to a professional course of teacher training (PGCE) and that some degree schemes may give comparatively little time and weighting to practical language work. Not all the degree schemes which neglect the language skills are of the traditional type. In some 'modern' schemes of study where excellent courses of contemporary descriptive linguistics and socio-linguistics (given naturally in English) are provided, comparatively little time is devoted to speaking and writing the language. In other words we are in an 'anything goes' situation and there is no guarantee that our new colleagues will have been given a balanced diet of oral and written work and of theoretical and practical language studies.

Among applied linguists and teachers there are widely differing views about the overt teaching of grammar but we would imagine that the vast majority would expect the teacher of a foreign language to possess a sound conscious knowledge and understanding of the morphology, syntax, semantics, phonology and phonetics of the contemporary forms of the language as well as of the conventions governing its appropriate use. Yet here again, because of the largely global assessment procedures and because each degree or certificate-granting institution is free to include or not include such matters in its teaching programme, there is no guarantee that the intending teacher will have reached an adequate level of understanding, nor indeed that he will have been given an adequate amount of instruction in all (or even in any) of these areas.

B. Study and experience of appropriate aspects of the foreign culture

In spite of global schemes of assessment over widely differing degree and certificate syllabuses, one thing that might reassure us would be the knowledge that all new teachers will at least have had the benefit of a structured year of study and practical experience of living in the foreign country. But once again although many will have spent a longer or a shorter period abroad, this is still not universally compulsory, nor when it is required is it always controlled and organised so as to provide the optimal benefit to the student.

C. The teacher's knowledge of the formal structure and functions of English

Normally English will be the mother tongue both of the teachers and the pupils, but even when this is not the case it will nevertheless be their second language and the language of instruction in the school. This being so it would seem reasonable to us to assert that the teacher who does not possess a conscious knowledge of how the English language functions is lacking one important pedagogical tool. In saying this we are not suggesting that the contrastive approach to foreign language teaching is of itself sufficient, nor are we accepting the claim that a contrastive analysis of the native and foreign languages will be able to predict and explain all or even the majority of errors in L2 learning. What we are claiming is that for the teacher at least, the ability to make comparisons and contrasts between the languages can be of considerable use in predicting likely areas of difficulty; facilitating error correction and explanation; preparing suitable teaching materials; and in integrating L1 and L2 learning and teaching. (Contrastive studies are here understood to include not only the formal structures of the two languages but also their functions and the differing views of the world they reflect.)

At present, however, there is no guarantee that the foreign language teacher in our schools will have had any linguistic training in English. Although most will have an 'O' level pass in English, some an 'A' level, and a few will have taken English as a main or subsidiary subject at college or university, it is quite possible that all these courses will have been mainly concerned with literary studies.

D. Initial professional training and the probationary year
(a) Aims and articulation of training

Turning now to the professional training phase — the one-year PGCE or the professional and curriculum components of the Certificate and BEd courses — we can see that the present system confronts the trainers of our foreign language teachers with the virtually impossible task of providing in the totally inadequate amount of time at their disposal, not only the multi-disciplinary professional training that they and most applied linguists would agree was necessary, but also the task of filling in the gaps in the trainees' basic linguistic knowledge and skills.

This situation is made even more difficult for our teacher trainers since in Britain, unlike some other European countries, we do not require our teachers once qualified ever to take any further in-service training. Those responsible for teacher training therefore feel compelled somehow to attempt in that short initial training period, to equip the new recruit with all he will need in the way of training for the rest of his professional life.

And then there is the 'lottery', 'farce', 'chaos' of the probationary year — it has been called all these things and many more. If only our teacher trainers could count on that year to supplement the initial training phase this would ease their difficulties considerably. However under the present arrangements it is purely a matter of luck whether the probationary teacher receives a great deal of encouragement, support and further training or virtually none — not that in one sense he need worry since about 99 per cent of probationary teachers are accepted into the profession.

On two counts (the fact that in this country in-service training is neither compulsory nor rewarded and the fact that the arrangements for the probationary year are uncoordinated, haphazard and chaotic) we can sympathise with the teacher training institutions and agree that they cannot be held responsible.

There are, however, some other problems connected with certain aspects of initial training which it would be proper to ask them to solve. We will mention just four areas where it seems to us that immediate improvements could be effected, namely in the arrangements made for:

  (i) teaching practice and its assessment;
 (ii) the specialist training of teachers of the so-called 'minority' languages (ie modern foreign languages other than French);
(iii) the bringing together of intending teachers of modern foreign languages and of the mother tongue to study some of the language learning and language teaching problems they will have to face in the classroom;
(iv) the involvement of practising teachers in the schools in the initial training of student teachers.

(b) Teaching Practice and its assessment

At present because of the grace and favour basis on which teacher training institutions receive an allocation of teaching practice places for their students, not all of them can give a firm guarantee that each student will be given supervised practice in teaching his particular foreign language at the particular level (junior, middle, secondary) he wishes to specialise in. Some colleges, for example, may not be able to find enough (or indeed any) places in junior schools where French is taught. Some university departments of education may not be able to provide teaching practice opportunites in Spanish, German, Russian or Italian even though they may have accepted for training students specialising in one or more of these languages. Also, because of the way teaching practice is organised in some colleges there is no firm guarantee that even if appropriate practice has been arranged, the student will be supervised and assessed by a member of staff who is a specialist in the foreign language. It is of course true that many teacher training institutions make perfectly adequate teaching practice arrangements for all their students, but the question that we are once again asking is whether a serious profession should countenance the possibility that some might not.

(c) The training of teachers of the 'minority' languages

In the case of intending teachers of German, Italian, Russian and Spanish not only is there no guarantee that they will be given teaching practice in these languages, there is also no guarantee that they will be given their professional training by tutors possessing the appropriate specialist qualifications and experience. There is no question, of course, of any deceit about this, the intending teacher of the minority

108

language is (or should be) aware of the situation when he applies to a particular institution where the necessary facilities or staffing are not available. Nevertheless, even if the student is willing to accept a place in these circumstances, is it right that we should give our tacit approval to a system which permits some of our future teachers of Spanish, Russian, etc, to be trained by tutors who are not specialists in these languages and to complete their training without being given relevant teaching practice opportunities?

(d) 'The space between'

As things stand at present, specialist teachers of modern foreign languages and of English as the mother tongue more often than not receive their education and training in quasi-isolation from each other (even within the same institution), without ever being brought together to study common problems of language learning and language teaching, and indeed without ever having their attention drawn even to the possibility that as teachers of language they might have problems in common. In these circumstances it is hardly surprising that in so many schools there is very little in the way of professional dialogue (let alone collaboration) between the teachers of English and their modern languages colleagues, and that for teachers and learners alike, the two subjects remain isolated in watertight compartments. Even the 'semi-specialist' teacher of French in the junior or middle school will only too often have received his foreign language method training and his English method training in two quite separate courses with little or no attempt to relate them. And in these circumstances too, it is hardly surprising that French in the primary school has sometimes appeared to stick out like a sore thumb. Although in some of our teacher training institutions arrangements are made for students preparing to teach foreign languages to come together for part of their language teaching training with students intending to specialise in teaching English, this is far from being the general practice (see section 4 above). This too often results in foreign language teachers taking up their first posts without any idea of the aims, content and methodology of the English component of the curriculum and with no expectations of being able to collaborate with their English colleagues in joint projects for the mutual benefit of both teachers and learners. This situation is, we suggest, one we should view with concern and as part of our compaign for a more professional approach to the training of language teachers we ought to encourage the development of links between the two groups (or rather three groups, if the institution also provides training for teachers of English as a foreign language). Briefly the grounds for asserting that such links would be desirable from the foreign language point of view are:

(i) foreign language teaching would be more effective if it took into account the pupils' linguistic development and learning strategies in the native language and if its aims were more closely related to those of mother-tongue teaching;

(ii) foreign language learners would find their task easier and more rewarding if they could relate it to other learning experiences and other areas of the curriculum;

(iii) foreign language teachers would be more thoroughly prepared to deal with their pupils' linguistic problems if they were more aware of first language acquisition processes and of the development of language skills in the mother tongue lessons.

We would similarly claim that mother-tongue teaching would benefit from this closer association, particularly but not exclusively, with regard to the sometimes neglected linguistic skills element of the teaching programme. However, this is doubtless a more controversial claim and best left to the teachers of English to justify or refute from their own point of view.

(e) The involvement of serving teachers in initial training

The great majority of the tutors and lecturers who are responsible for the training of foreign language teachers are themselves experienced teachers. However, unless there has recently been a dramatic change, the majority of them gained their practical teaching experience in selective secondary schools and consequently have little direct personal experience of teaching foreign languages in junior, middle or comprehensive schools. This is, of course, a problem of which they are well aware and to their great credit many of them have undertaken teaching in such schools in addition to their many other heavy commitments. It is also becoming more common for teacher-tutors to be employed to supplement the permanent full-time lecturers and tutors and sometimes joint appointments are made to the LEA and university or college.

Nevertheless, this is far from being a universal custom and if, as we have suggested, one of our basic principles should be that an adequate professional training must include supervision and guidance from experienced practitioners who are themselves teaching or who have recently taught in schools of the type for which the trainee is being prepared, we are once more given cause for concern. We would further suggest that this basic principle will not be met entirely if the students' official contacts with experienced teachers are limited to the teaching practice phase of his training (even though this in itself would be an improvement on what now happens in some cases). The involvement of serving teachers should, we believe, go further than this: not only should the student go into the schools (for observation and practice) but the school teachers should go into the training institutions to meet the students (and staff) and play a part in the training programme both before and after teaching practice.

(f) In-service training

Whatever criticisms one might make of the provisions for in-service training for teachers of foreign languages it would be difficult to maintain that insufficient courses are offered (in 1975, for example, 27 out of 42 courses were cancelled for lack of applicants), or that there is insufficient variety (colleges, UDEs, polytechnics, university language departments, DES, HMI, language advisers, teachers' centres, the professional associations, etc, all offer in-service courses of one kind or another). Nor does it seem that there is any general dissatisfaction with the quality of the instruction provided. What is basically wrong is that in-service training is neither compulsory nor rewarded and that the provision of this training is fragmented, uncoordinated and unevenly distributed in the various parts of the country. The result is that many of the teachers who are most in need of further training do not bother to enroll or simply cannot afford to. We are not advocating a monolithic, uniform training system, but surely it would be sensible to make some in-service training both compulsory and free during the 40-odd years of a teacher's professional life. And would it not also be sensible to coordinate to some degree at least the efforts of the large number of agencies involved in in-service training?

There is also a need for in-service training courses specially designed to prepare teachers for promotion to headships of department of modern languages in the schools, and we are glad that this is being advocated by HMI. We would, in fact, like to go further and make it a requirement for promotion, but of course before one could get to that position it would be necessary to specify what are the duties and responsibilities of such posts — something which strangely enough is practically never done.

So yet again (and this is our last example) we find that so much is left to chance that it becomes difficult to maintain we are making serious efforts to maintain and improve professional standards.

6. Conclusions

The most optimistic conclusion that we can come to is that while many of our future specialist foreign language teachers will have received an appropriate education and training, we cannot be sure that all (or even the majority) will have attained what we could accept as minimal standards in all the necessary language skills and in all the relevant areas of knowledge. This is even more worrying since there is also an unknown number of teachers engaged in foreign language teaching, principally but not exclusively in junior and middle schools, whose only academic and professional qualifications in the foreign language and in foreign language teaching consist of a pass at CSE or 'O' level and a non-main course at college.

Thus the question is: should a self respecting profession continue to tolerate a situation which allows even the possibility that new recruits may be deficient in basic linguistic skills and knowledge? Would the British Medical Association, for example, (to say nothing of the public) tolerate a similar situation when all they could honestly claim would be that they were only reasonably certain that a large proportion of doctors had received an appropriate training and possessed those basic medical skills the exercise of their profession demanded?

The first step we should like to see taken is the bringing together in one professional body all language teachers (mother tongue teachers and teachers of foreign or second languages) at all levels of the educational system. One of the main functions of such a body would be to make its view known on the education and training of new recruits to the profession. It should also insist on having a decisive voice in determining and monitoring the standards of training programmes and trainees' performance. However, since language teachers are teachers first and subject specialists second, this body should see its functions as primarily related to the specialist language teaching aspects of the students' education and training, ie it would most appropriately become a constituent section of a British Teaching Council (or some similar general governing body). And as such it would, we hope, add its voice to the growing demand for a fully graduate teaching profession with high professional standards, eg by pressing for the integration of the probationary year into a two-year initial training period (following a suitable three-or-four-year undergraduate education) and for a minimum of compulsory, free and rewarded in-service training (including obligatory training for posts of responsibility.

Detailed proposals are beyond the scope of this paper, but we would like to suggest that the first year of the combined initial training/probationary period should be mainly (but not exclusively) college or university based and the second year mainly (but not exclusively) school-based. We would also suggest that the probationary teacher should be paid half a teacher's salary and half a postgraduate student's grant and that he should only count as occupying half a post for staffing establishment purposes (James suggested merely that he should have only two-thirds of a normal teaching load, a suggestion which, although inadequate as a solution to the problem, has so far turned out to be too radical and expensive for most LEAs to implement). Again, without going into details we would hope that this newly constituted body of language teachers would, among the first tasks it undertook,

(a) specify the minimum level of attainment in the various foreign language skills an intending member of the profession should possess and institute nationally administered tests which eventually it would be compulsory for the new teacher to pass before being given a 'licence' to teach a foreign language, in addition, of course, to passing his Bachelor's degree and professional teaching qualification;

(b) urge the making of the year abroad a necessary part of foreign language teachers' education and training and suggest (eventually prescribe) certain minimum requirements for a properly structured programme of study and learning experience during the stay in the foreign country;

(c) obtain the necessary authorisation to approve (or not to approve) undergraduate syllabuses as being suitable for intending foreign language teachers in the same way as the College of Speech Therapists and the British Psychological Society do at present. Universities and colleges must, of course, be free to teach what they want to teach and to teach in the ways they judge best, but we also should be free to approve certain syllabuses as being appropriate for our purpose and not to approve others;

(d) similarly obtain authority to approve or not approve the foreign language methodology components of the professional training syllabuses and the arrangements for teaching practice and its assessment (including the assessment of the probationary year).

It would of course, equally be the concern of this body to take similar steps with regard to the education and training of mother tongue and teachers of English as a foreign language.

There is little that is new in the proposals made in this paper, many similar suggestions have already been made. The main object has been to make a plea for united action by existing members of the language teaching profession in defence of their profession. We have been content for far too long to rely on others to regulate our affairs and the time has come to insist on having a decisive voice in the conduct of our own profession.

But first we must decide among ourselves exactly what we want.

Bibliography to part 2

Centre for Information on Language Teaching and Research. CILT Reports and Papers 10: *The space between: English and foreign languages at school*. CILT, 1974.

Centre for Information on Language Teaching and Research. CILT Reports and Papers 15: *The continuing training of modern language teachers*. CILT, 1976.

Committee for Inquiry into Reading and the Use of English. *A language for life*. HMSO, 1975. (The Bullock Report.)

Department of Education and Science. *Teacher education and training*. HMSO, 1972. (The James Report.)

Her Majesty's Inspectorate of Schools. *Modern languages in comprehensive schools*. HMSO, 1977. (Matters for discussion 3.)

Spicer, A, and Riddy, D.C. *Initial training of teachers of modern languages*. E.J. Arnold, 1977.